Against the Wind

"Incredible Journeys" Books
Available from Whitehorse Press

Ron Ayres: *Against the Wind*
Ted Simon: *Jupiter's Travels*
Robert Fulton: *One Man Caravan*
Ed Culberson: *Obsessions Die Hard*
Danny Liska: *Two Wheels to Adventure*
William Carroll: *Two Wheels to Panama*
Christopher Hunt: *Sparring With Charlie*
Robert Auburn: *The Endless Ride*
Che Guevara: *Motorcycle Diaries*
Jim Rogers: *Investment Biker*
Dave Barr: *Riding the Edge*

Against the Wind

A Rider's Account of the Incredible Iron Butt Rally

Ron Ayres

Whitehorse Press
North Conway, New Hampshire

Unless otherwise noted, photographs are by the author.

You may contact the author through the Internet at:
   ron@ronayres.com

We recognize that some words, model names, and designations
mentioned herein are the property of the trademark holder.
We use them for identification purposes only.

An Incredible Journeys Book.
Published May 1997 by
   Whitehorse Press
   P.O. Box 60
   North Conway, New Hampshire 03860 USA
   Phone: 603-356-6556 or 800-531-1133
   Fax: 603-356-6590
   E-mail: WhitehorsePress@compuserve.com

Whitehorse Press is a trademark of Kennedy Associates.

ISBN 1-884313-09-4

5 4 3 2

Printed in the United States of America

Dedication

To my mother, Marian Anne Ayres—who, after she reads this, probably won't let me ride motorcycles any more.

"The Iron Butt is an endurance rally, and it's about getting on the machine and staying on for eleven days. The riders see a good portion of the contiguous U.S. They see it in the ever-brightening dawn of day, the blazing afternoon sunshine, the golden haze of sunset, and the cold darkness of night. They experience the Rocky Mountains and turn up their electric vests as temperatures drop to 30 degrees. They experience the reds and browns of the southwestern desert and survive 115-degree temperatures as blasts of hot air envelop their leather or Gore-Tex-clad bodies. They sip fluids from tubes from packs on their backs in an attempt to stay hydrated and to keep their attention on their ever-changing environment. They wipe face shields clear of driving rain and brace themselves against persistent winds as they ride the fringes of hurricanes threatening to alter their course to the next checkpoint. What is the mystique that surrounds the Iron Butt Rally?"

From *"How We Spent Our Summer Vacation: We Rode Hard, Went Far and Kept Smilin',"* Karol Patzer, *BMW Owners News*

Contents

The answer could be, in this most sublimely solitary of sports, ironically a question of companionship. The riders rarely see each other, dancing as they do across the country in chaotic, Brownian motion. They're not talking to anyone, except maybe to themselves. If they're not riding, sleeping in the saddle on the side of the road, or eating dinner while standing next to a gas pump at three o'clock in the morning, then they're just wasting time.

But think of the end. Think how glorious it will be to get off the bike and not have to count the minutes until you have to strap yourself onto it again. When you turn off the key for the last time, there aren't 100 people on earth who can seriously appreciate what you have undergone. About 40 of them will show up at a motel west of Salt Lake City, looking as pounded as you do. They are the only ones who really know. The rest of us can only guess. *You ride this endless ride to be one of them.*

Ron Ayres's book tries to explain the fascination of long distance riders—an even more unusual subset of an already unusual breed—with this draining, lonely contest. Like all good sagas, its heroes and villains compete against themselves, the imponderable fates, and a ceaselessly ticking clock. Here, told from the point of view of a participant, the unravelling of human souls proceeds in almost embarrassing clarity. Only a chosen few escape unharmed; the rest, victims of the thousand ills that flesh is heir to, fall along the wayside.

Ted Williams once said that the hardest task in sports was to hit a baseball thrown by a major league pitcher. Maybe, but as good as he was, Ted Williams never ran the Iron Butt Rally.

—Bob Higdon

Acknowledgments

The author is extremely grateful for the enthusiastic support of the contestants of the 1995 Iron Butt Rally. More than two dozen riders provided material to support the writing of this book. *Against the Wind* could not have been written without their help and would not have been written without their encouragement.

I would like to thank by name the riders who responded to my request for information about their 1995 Iron Butt experience. The list includes Steve Attwood, Harold Brooks, Jerry Clemmons, Jim Culp, Gary Eagan, Charles Elberfeld, Horst Haak, Martin Hildebrandt, Suzy Johnson, Marty Jones, Morris Kruemcke, Phyllis Lang, Tom Loegering, Steve Losofsky, Ron Major, Eddie Metz, Rick Morrison, Mike Murphy, Karol Patzer, Jesse Pereboom, Hank Rowland, Rick Shrader, Gregg Smith, Michael Stockton, Willie Thommes, and Boyd Young.

A special thanks is due to Rallymaster Steve Chalmers and to Mike Kneebone, Chairman of the Iron Butt Association, for agreeing to review the material for accuracy and for offering suggestions for its improvement. I would also like to thank Mike for permitting me to use information from the Iron Butt Association web page, especially Bob Higdon's daily Internet postings.

Finally, I would like to thank my wife, Barbara, and my sister-in-law, Roberta Robinson, for countless hours spent in developing suggestions for improving the book. Roberta has been my single most important critic, offering invaluable suggestions for the organization of the material and for the improvement of my writing style. The project would have been far less successful without her generous help.

1

Birth of a Passion

Getting Started

Serendipity or Destiny?

It wasn't yet noon on a warm spring morning in 1991 when I stopped at a rest area at the entrance to the Talimena Scenic Drive in eastern Oklahoma. As I was parking my motorcycle, a rider descended the steep grade leading toward the termination point of the picturesque road where I stood. When he saw me we exchanged waves. He pulled into the parking lot, parked his motorcycle next to mine, and dismounted. As he removed his helmet and gloves, I commented on the great riding weather and asked about his destination.

"My name is Mike Kneebone," he said as he extended his hand. "I'm on my way to Dallas. I'm the rallymaster for the Iron Butt Rally in August and I'm laying out the route. I think this scenic drive will make a great bonus location."

I recognized the rider's name immediately. Mike was president of the Iron Butt Association and one of the world's most renowned endurance riders. He shares a Guinness world record with riding legend Fran Crane for visiting all 48 states in six days, 13 hours, and 21 minutes. His punishing road tests have inspired two BMW advertisements.

I also recognized the name of the rally. The Iron Butt is the most notable motorcycle endurance riding competition in the world. Top riders travel more than 11,000 miles in 11 days while visiting checkpoints from one end of the United States to the other. They do this with virtually no sleep, little nourishment, and while enduring extremes of heat, cold, and any other obstacles that fate contrives. The event isn't a race. It's a test of mental toughness, determination, strategy, and resolve. Speed is far less important than the ability to manage stress and formulate a winning plan at the sheer limits of human endurance. For many riders, the goal is simply to finish.

The rally takes place every two years and is arguably "The World's Toughest Motorcycle Competition," a term that has become the rally's catch phrase. Riders everywhere recognize it as one of the most demanding motorcycle endurance events ever conceived. Considering that only 26 riders from around the world would participate in the 1991 rally, I astonished Mike when I introduced myself as an entrant.

"Are you planning to use the Harley in the rally?" Mike asked as he walked to my full dresser touring motorcycle parked at the curb.

"No," I answered. "I wanted a nice lazy ride today. When I bring my BMW K100RS up here I can't seem to keep the speed down through the curves. But I'm planning to use it in the rally. If *you* had to choose between the two motorcycles for the rally, what would your choice be?"

I had never participated in an endurance rally and was hungry for information. Mike was generous—almost eager—to share it. This was my first opportunity to talk with an experienced Iron Butt competitor and I wanted to make the most of it. Considering Mike's accomplishments, I wouldn't have expected him to be so low-key. I liked his warm, friendly manner immediately. I sensed that he didn't want to snub either of my choices. I liked the guy even more.

"The main thing is that you should ride a motorcycle that's comfortable while cruising just a bit over legal speed limits. I

Mike Kneebone at Prudhoe Bay, Alaska

have a dresser too, but I find the engine noise annoying at 80 mph or more. I love BMWs, but I need something with more protection from the elements than the K100RS provides," he commented.

We talked some more. He expressed concern about having disclosed a bonus location and suggested he would consider dropping it from the list of bonus opportunities. We then agreed to meet in Sparks, Nevada, the starting point for the 1991 event. As he departed for Dallas, I headed across the breathtaking drive that snakes its way across the peaks of the Kiamichi Mountains and through the Ouachita National Forest to Mena, Arkansas, nearly 50 miles to the east. I tried to let the significance of the chance encounter register. I couldn't wait to tell my wife, Barb, about the coincidental meeting.

During the next several years I came to know Mike better, through letters and phone conversations about the Iron Butt. On one occasion he was our house guest while passing through Dallas. I recall the caution he displayed when first introduced to Barb. He was reluctant to discuss the rally until he determined her attitude about it.

I am blessed with a wife who has always been supportive, even encouraging, about my interest in endurance riding. She participated eagerly in our conversation.

"Are you planning to ride the rally just to finish, or do you think you'll be a contender?" Mike asked during dinner. I don't remember what I mumbled in response, but I didn't want to sound presumptuous by suggesting that I was capable of competing with "the world's toughest motorcycle riders." At that point, I didn't know if I could.

Discovering The Iron Butt

I always had a dormant interest in motorcycles. In 1987, at 44, I indulged myself and bought my first motorcycle, a Harley-Davidson Low Rider. My mother was visiting when I rode the motorcycle home and pulled into the driveway. As a youth, I was a thrill-seeking daredevil who subjected her to many sleepless nights. She often worried that I wouldn't survive my childhood. When I married and became a father for the first time, she

Author and wife Barbara "on tour" in Colorado at Engineer Pass along Colorado's "Million Dollar Highway."

began to relax, believing she had witnessed my passage into adulthood. Now she wasn't sure. After watching me park the motorcycle, she quietly returned to her room, locked the door, and cried.

I subscribed to several motorcycle magazines and became aware of a small group of riders who share an obsession for riding extraordinary distances. I read an article about the Iron Butt Rally which included a picture of Fran Crane, who had finished second in the 1987 rally. The endurance riding seed fell on fertile ground. I became intrigued with the idea of riding up to 1,000 miles per day, 11 days in a row. I wanted to find out more.

I learned that participants include motorcyclists from around the world. Occupations range from neurosurgeon to lawyer, and include business executives, truck drivers, pilots, engineers, and law enforcement officers. The riders earn points for visiting one checkpoint after another within a specified time. They earn additional points for visiting "bonus" locations, which they learn of only just before each leg of the rally to make advance planning impossible. Each leg includes many more bonus locations than a rider could possibly visit in the time allotted to reach the next checkpoint—so careful strategizing is necessary to squeeze in as many as possible.

The value of bonuses increases dramatically as the rally progresses. Generous bonuses are available to riders able to preserve the energy they need to ride hard during the closing days of the rally. It might be necessary to ride 500 miles to snatch 500 points during the first day. A week later, a ride of the same distance might yield three times as many points. The rider who collects the most points wins. And the coveted prize? Nothing more than an inexpensive trophy—and a feeling of unmatched satisfaction.

Before putting the first 1,000 miles on my first motorcycle, I took off for Colorado with John, a friend who borrowed his brother's Yamaha 650. We spent more than a week in the Colorado Rockies and the Monument Valley area of Utah. We were pleased with ourselves the first time we logged 600 miles in one day.

I mentioned my interest in the Iron Butt to John during our trip. I still remember his words: "Ron, look at how totally fried we are after a 500-mile ride. Even if we *could* do 1,000 miles in a day, can you imagine what it must be like to get up in the morning and know you have to do it ten more times in a row?"

My love of motorcycles developed into a passion as I purchased my second, third, and fourth machines. Counting the motorcycles owned by two of my three sons, we once crammed six of them into our garage in Plano, Texas.

Gradually, I progressed to the point of riding an occasional 1,000-mile day. Barb's mother lived in Hatfield, Wisconsin, at the time, and Barb visited her for a few weeks each summer. I came to use this as an excuse to make the 1,150-mile trip on the Harley. I almost always made the journey from Plano in less than 24 hours.

I had submitted an application to ride in the 1988 Iron Butt Rally, intending to ride the Harley. According to Mike Kneebone, the organizers at that time mishandled the promotion and registration, and the rally was canceled.

As my interest in endurance riding grew, I learned none of my bikes was ideal for the Iron Butt. Only one Harley-Davidson rider had completed the event thus far, and he didn't finish well. My Low Rider was a great motorcycle, but it wasn't suited for the challenges the Iron Butt would present. This provided an excuse for me to buy my first BMW, the K100RS.

Each time I rode a motorcycle I became Walter Mitty, fantasizing about riding the Iron Butt. I couldn't get the challenge out of my mind. Whenever I purchased clothing or motorcycle equipment, I first considered its suitability for the rally. Even a visit to my optometrist was an occasion to discuss the type of riding I was planning. I bought glasses and contact lenses that would be most appropriate. I sought opportunities to do as much endurance riding as I could, often riding 1,000 miles per day on trips to Big Bend National Park in southwest Texas, the bayous of Louisiana, or the Ouachita Mountains in Arkansas.

I entered the 1991 rally. When unforeseen business issues interfered, I had to withdraw. The Sparks-based rally would be the first, but not last, Iron Butt I would enter and then skip.

I had been president of a small management consulting company. At the beginning of 1993, my partners and I sold the business to a large information technology company that I had worked for 13 years earlier. Several months later, I moved to Spain to manage a large consulting engagement for the company. I had registered for the 1993 rally before moving to Europe, and I scheduled my trip home months in advance, but two weeks before the rally, another unexpected business conflict arose. Once again, I was an Iron Butt no-show.

When registration for the 1995 rally opened, I entered once more. The popularity of the rally had grown as more motorcyclists became interested in endurance riding. Only 60 riders were selected from the more than 300 who tried to register. I was one of them. I vowed to participate in this rally at any cost.

By 1995 I had moved to São Paulo, Brazil, and was directing my company's management consulting business in Latin America. I continued communicating with Mike, who repeatedly asked if I would make it back for the rally. In the meantime, I teased him about coming to South America to ride through the Andes.

I was so sure I would participate in the 1995 rally that I began looking for a new motorcycle. I still enjoyed my K100RS, but knew that I was ready for a motorcycle with more protection from the elements. I selected another BMW, a K1100LT.

The Number 1 starting position is traditionally reserved for some deserving rider. In 1993, Rick Shrader received the honor after having the Iron Butt logo tattooed on his arm, an ultimate expression of his dedication to the rally. In 1995, I was facetiously awarded the honor in recognition of my many no-shows.

In January 1995, after the roster had been prepared, contestants received a letter from Mike in which he summarized the backgrounds of the participants. The letter included a humorous anecdote about each entrant. Of me, Mike wrote:

> *"Perhaps some last-minute career or family problem will keep a few of you from making it to the starting line. Before dropping out of the rally, I suggest you consult with rider number one: Ron Ayres. Ron has a high-stress executive style job and has paid to run the 1988, 1991, and 1993 Iron Butt Rallies. If you want to know about the financial and psychological pain of dropping out of the Iron Butt, talk to the expert (Ron's record of three tries earned him the number one position on the roster)! That is, if you can find him. The last we heard, Ron is hopelessly lost in a small South American country doing covert consulting work."*

There was a hand-written note in the margin: "Ron, if anyone should call, please tell them that we are RUTHLESS! Mike."

I returned to the United States from Brazil less than a week before the Tuesday, August 29, start of the rally. This scarcely left me time to prepare the motorcycle before leaving for Salt Lake City, where the Iron Butt would begin and end.

I departed Plano at 10:30 on Sunday morning for the 1,300-mile ride to Salt Lake City. My schedule provided a little more than one day to make the trip, and I was looking forward to the warm-up ride. I knew it would allow me to indulge in the two things I enjoy most about motorcycling.

The first is riding overnight without stopping to sleep. There is something fascinating about continuing to ride after the sun has descended on one side of the motorcycle and continuing to ride until it rises again on the opposite side. Knowing that the rest of the world sleeps while I ride all night is one of my most cherished experiences. This is why I loved my summer rides to Wisconsin.

The second is to stop to gaze at the universe, far from city lights that diminish the brightness and clarity of the stars. I prefer to do this when I'm alone and haven't seen other vehicles for a long time. I love the feeling of desolation that such a stop provides.

I took such a break in the Colorado mountains on the way to Utah. The road was totally deserted and dark, except for starlight. I couldn't see city lights, vehicle lights, or lights from any dwelling. Total silence, save the subdued chirping of insects. I relished this moment more than usual, because I knew that I couldn't enjoy such moments during the long-anticipated challenge that now lay only days ahead. My sense of contentment and well-being was disturbed only by an occasional twinge of uncertainty about whether I would measure up to the challenge.

The 1995 Iron Butt Rally, Base Route 8,796 Miles

S e p t e m b e r 1 9 9 5						
Mon	**Tue**	**Wed**	**Thur**	**Fri**	**Sat**	**Sun**
28 12:00 Check-in 4:00 Novice rider meeting 7:00 Rider dinner	29 4:00 Receive rally packets 5:00 Rally starts	30 3:00 Spokane window opens 5:00 Spokane window closes	31	1 10:00 San Diego window opens 12:00 San Diego window closes	2	3
4 6:00 Ft Laud. window opens 7:00 Ft Laud. window closes	5	6 6:00 Gorham window opens 8:00 Gorham window closes	7	8	9 5:00 S.L.C. window opens 7:00 S.L.C. window closes 7:00 Banquet	10
11	12	13	14	15	16	17
18	19	20	21	22	23	24
25	26	27	28	29	30	

2

The Gathering

Meeting the Riders

Before the Beginning

I arrived in Salt Lake City a little after 9:00 a.m. on Monday. Check-in would begin at noon. Other riders had already parked in a reserved area of the lot and were tinkering with motorcycles and renewing old acquaintances. Many had arrived a few

September 1995						
Mon	**Tue**	**Wed**	**Thur**	**Fri**	**Sat**	**Sun**
28	29	30	31	1	2	3
4	5	6	7	8	9	10
11	12	13	14	15	16	17
18	19	20	21	22	23	24
25	26	27	28	29	30	

days earlier, wanting to be rested for the start of the rally and welcoming the opportunity to visit with friends.

As I pulled into the area, a rider nodded and moved the barricade to let me pass and park my motorcycle inside the corral. I was already beginning to feel a part of something special. I located an available spot next to a blue K75, backed my bike into the parking spot, lifted the bike onto the center-stand, and turned to introduce myself. The rider, Ardys Kellerman, was making some adjustments to her motorcycle.

This would be Ardys Kellerman's second Iron Butt Rally. Seen here with her K75RT, Ardys had already won a number of BMW high-mileage contests.

Ardys, a grand-mother in her early 60s, was preparing for her second Iron Butt Rally. Prior to this rally, 63 riders had finished an Iron Butt. Only three were women, and one of them was Ardys. She had already managed a number of motorcycle-related accomplishments before entering the Iron Butt: In three consecutive years, Ardys finished first, second, and third in the woman's category of the BMW Motorcycle Owners of America annual "high mileage" contest. In her fourth year in the contest, she rode 50,089 miles in six months to finish first again, beating the second-place woman handily and losing to the top male rider by fewer than 1,500 miles.

I walked across the parking lot and into the office of the motel to register for my room. As I approached the check-in counter, the largest motorcyclist I had ever seen was waiting in line. At 6-foot-7 and 300 pounds, Mike "murf" Murphy (murf doesn't capitalize his nickname, a practice adopted from his favorite poet, ee cummings) overshadowed everyone in the lobby. "How the heck can a guy with those long legs be comfortable enough on any motorcycle to participate in this thing?" I wondered.

As surprised as I was to meet such an overwhelming partici-pant, I was even more surprised to learn that Dr. Murphy was a neurosurgeon at the St. Louis University Health Sciences Center. I wouldn't have expected a man with hands so huge to have the dexterity to operate on people's brains.

This was murf's first rally, but he seemed prepared, having made guaranteed reservations at motels along his intended route. Although locations of bonuses are undisclosed at the beginning of the rally, checkpoints and window times are pub-lished in advance.

Murf had also arranged to have clean underwear shipped to the checkpoints so that he could discard those he had already worn. I don't know if he had received advice from experienced riders, but I later learned that many riders use "disposable" clothing on rallies. They patronize the Goodwill Store or the Salvation Army to stock their wardrobes, then discard the clothing rather than launder it or carry it home.

Murf had undergone knee surgery just a few weeks before the rally. He was having some difficulty with his leg, and should have had a skin graft. He decided to forgo this aspect of the operation because the skin graft would have prevented him from sitting on a motorcycle with bent knee for the long hours required during the rally.

"I just looked at the bikes in the parking lot and I must be the only one here with a stock motorcycle," murf remarked.

"No, mine is stock too," I replied.

Iron Butt rules limit riders to a total capacity of eleven gallons of fuel, which is about five gallons more than motorcy-cles can carry when they leave the factory. Many riders equip their bikes with additional capacity. Murf would later have the ironic experience of providing fuel to a stranded rider whose bike was equipped with an auxiliary tank.

Brian Bush, President of Talk in Pictures, was with murf at the check-in counter. Brian came to Salt Lake City to produce a documentary video about the rally. He was also planning to ride the first two legs to experience firsthand the conditions encoun-tered by the riders. If Brian had been able to predict the bizarre

1995 Iron Butt Rallymaster Steve Chalmers is looking forward to the 1997 Iron Butt Rally as a competitor.

series of events that would screw up the production of his video, he probably would have stayed home.

Rendezvous with the Rallymaster

After a short nap, I returned to the parking lot to check in. The instructions I received before leaving home had suggested it would save everyone time if riders would take required items to the check-in location. These included a first-aid kit, tire repair, flashlight, proof of insurance, helmet, riding boots, and license. Upon showing these items, I would receive instructions for performing an odometer check so that my odometer readings could be reconciled with the official odometer used by rallymaster Steve Chalmers when the course was laid out.

Although I had spoken to Steve by phone, this was our first meeting in person. An ex-Marine, Steve grew up in southern California and moved to Salt Lake City over ten years ago. He claims to have almost 40 years of riding experience. He claims he started riding four months before he was conceived.

For several years, Steve has conducted the Utah 1088 Rally, a fundraiser for Project Hope, an initiative sponsored by the Utah Highway Patrol to benefit disadvantaged children. Highway Patrol officers assist Steve with technical inspection of the motorcycles at this annual 24-hour endurance rally. Decals with the Utah Highway Patrol star are placed on the rear of motorcycles as technical inspection is completed. Steve wears these decals on the back of his motorcycle and on the back of his helmet. At least once, the decals helped him avoid a ticket. "While driving through Texas one night a bit over the speed limit, a car began following closely behind me," he said. "I was tired and wasn't paying attention and didn't suspect that this was a trooper. I was startled when I heard the voice of the Texas State Trooper booming over his PA system, 'Okay, son, I see what you do for a living, but if you don't slow down, you're gonna go to jail.' "

Steve Chalmers, who founded the Motorcycle Endurance Rider Association (MERA), is to MERA what Mike Kneebone is to the Iron Butt Association: founder and president.

Although both organizations promote endurance riding, they each have their own twists. The Iron Butt Association discourages speeding, refuses to acknowledge or promote records involving speed, and emphasizes safety. It's the Iron Butt that sometimes attracts "novelty riders" in addition to hard-core enthusiasts. Many riders, especially those interested in gaining recognition for establishing records, favor MERA. Some MERA events are "by invitation only" to riders who have successfully competed in other events.

These two icons of endurance riding have different riding styles. Kneebone loves to ride but retired from competitive endurance riding after being first to break the 50 hour barrier in the New York to San Francisco Guinness world record and being the first finisher of the 50cc Quest by riding cross-country in less than 50 hours. Chalmers, on the other hand, continues to participate in rallies. He loves riding in them as much as he enjoys staging them. He finished sixth in the 1993 Iron Butt Rally, almost always finishes in the top ten, and has never failed to finish a rally that he has entered.

Rick "Swamp Thing" Shrader being interviewed before the rally. The 1995 Iron Butt would be Rick's third attempt.

Cast of Characters

After completing my odometer check, I returned to the parking lot to meet more of the riders. It didn't take long to confirm that the rally attracts riders from a wide variety of backgrounds.

When I met Rick Shrader, a/k/a "Swamp Thing," I assumed from his appearance that he must be a Harley pilot. Rick's appearance approaches that of the "biker" stereotype. He has long hair, a matching long gray beard, and arms covered with tattoos, including one with the Iron Butt logo affirming his passion for the rally. But Rick's ride for this rally was a BMW.

Rick started riding in 1964. While stationed in Germany with the Air Force he purchased a '52 BSA Golden Flash, upon which he had his first date with his future wife, Jean. He had ridden a motorcycle through most of Europe, including Yugoslavia, Scotland, Belgium, the Czech Republic, and Norway. Rick was the first American to be Meritum in the Federation Internationale Motocycliste (FIM), an honor bestowed on riders attending five of the annual conferences hosted by this leading international motorcycling organization.

This would be Rick's third attempt to finish the Iron Butt. In 1991 he dumped his motorcycle into a swamp, for which he picked up the nickname "Swamp Thing." Two years later, he dropped out before the second checkpoint, a victim of engine problems and heat fatigue.

Homely Honda

I stepped back from the long line of parked motorcycles to take a snapshot of the assembled machinery. As I surveyed the collection of bikes, I caught sight of a Honda Helix single-cylinder motor scooter hiding among the larger, high-speed motorcycles. The homely little thing looked as though it was trying to remain inconspicuous, to not have its presence among the larger machines questioned.

I soon learned that the Helix belonged to Ed Otto, who had competed in 1993. His 250cc Honda was fundamentally a motor scooter with about 13 horsepower, less than most riding lawnmowers. A successful finish would earn him a place in Iron Butt history for finishing the rally on the smallest motorcycle.

Ed may have been riding a novelty vehicle, but he was taking the rally seriously. He had secured the sponsorship of

Ed Otto rode his Honda Helix, "Floppy," on the rally. The Helix, with less horsepower than many riding lawnmowers, was the smallest vehicle entered.

Motorcycle Consumer News, which provided the Helix. He had a custom-made rack built for a five-gallon auxiliary fuel tank, was carrying spare tires, and had plenty of storage for food and water. Later, a crowd of spectators gathered around the scooter. He and "Floppy" would receive similar attention over the next two weeks at checkpoints in Spokane, San Diego, Fort Lauderdale, and Gorham.

Ron and Karen McAteer were back, hoping to make Iron Butt history as the first couple to complete the rally riding two-up. Ron's sport-touring Honda ST1100 motorcycle wasn't nearly as comfortable as some of the motorcycles ridden by the solo riders.

Other returning Iron Butt veterans included Gary Gottfredson, Skip Ciccarelli, and Doug Stover.

Martin Hildebrandt shipped his Honda ST1100 "Pan Galactica" to the United States from his home in Germany. This was his first trip to the United States.

The Teutonic Threat

Murf asked if I had seen the high-tech machine that Martin Hildebrandt had shipped from Germany. "The thing uses satellite tracking to help him determine where he is," murf said.

I found the tall bearded German tinkering with his black Honda ST1100. He had shipped the bike from his home in Hanover, Germany, arriving nearly a week before the rally on the same Lufthansa flight from Germany to Chicago. He came farther than any other rider.

The Iron Butt would be Martin's first endurance rally. Until now, he had never competed in an endurance rally or ridden a 1,000-mile day. He had also never been in the United States.

Martin was visiting friends he had never met and had never spoken to before. He had been communicating with them via CompuServe (CIS), swapping e-mail with motorcycle enthusiasts around the world. He was to be the house guest of fellow "CISsies" in the Chicago suburb of Northbrook.

Martin, owner of a software development company, had mounted a personal computer on the motorcycle between the handlebars. He also had installed Pan-Galactica, a Global Positioning System (GPS) with a heads-up map display and CD-based mapping software that allowed him to plot his position accurately at any time. Presumably, this setup would compensate for the disadvantage of negotiating the highways of an unfamiliar land.

The Texans
In addition to Brian Bush from Corpus Christi, a number of other Texans also came for the rally. One of the most colorful riders of the group was Morris Kruemcke, a Gold Wing rider from Houston. Morris had a reputation for staying on the motorcycle for long, long periods without stopping. He was the only rider we knew to equip his motorcycle with a crude funnel device that allowed him to relieve himself without stopping. Morris claimed that the *real* advantage of the device was not that it eliminated frequent stops, but that it eliminated the tendency some riders have to dehydrate themselves by not drinking enough fluids.

Morris once equipped his motorcycle with a capacity of nearly 40 gallons and rode a distance of 1,220 miles without stopping. He claimed to have already logged more than 100 days of 1,000 or more miles. He won the five-day Run What You Brung Rally in 1994 with 6,700 miles under his belt.

Morris told me that a few years earlier he had fulfilled a longtime dream when he rode the entire length of the Alaska

Highway in less than 24 hours. The trip from Dawson Creek, British Columbia, to Fairbanks, Alaska, was nearly 1,300 miles long. "When I got there, I could swear that I heard a voice from above, saying, 'Who cares?'," Morris guffawed.

Marty Jones, a law enforcement officer and airplane pilot from San Angelo, Texas, was back for his second try at finishing the rally. Marty's primary mission is to stop drugs from coming across our southern borders. He tracks aircraft to their landing spots, then arrests the pilots. He also performs airborne surveillance of suspicious vehicles on the ground. Occasionally, he gets an opportunity to work in one of five foreign countries, interdicting foreign targets. When he isn't working on the more exciting stuff, he investigates money laundering operations.

When Marty attempted the Iron Butt in 1993, he totaled his motorcycle in West Virginia, breaking his leg in the process. He rode aggressively for eight days and didn't finish. This time he planned to ride more conservatively. He knew his wife would be unhappy to hear about his plan to enter again, so he didn't discuss it until six months before the rally.

I approached Eddie Metz, a fellow Texan from Grapevine who finished fourth in 1993. A mechanic with Delta Airlines, he had recently installed an auxiliary fuel tank in the rear luggage compartment of his Gold Wing. As we talked, Eddie asked if I had a strategy. I returned a blank stare, slightly embarrassed that I didn't have a ready answer. "Well, it's probably just as well to get on out there and just see what you can do," Eddie continued, helping me off the hook.

Dennis Searcy, a boilermaker and welder from Angleton, rounded out the Texas contingent. Dennis was one of only five contestants riding a Harley-Davidson.

A few Oklahomans were present too. Quiet and well-mannered Michael Stockton, a plant technician from Oklahoma City, looks like a man who spends a lot of time in the gym pumping iron when he isn't riding. Although he has ridden motorcycles since he was 14 and has done numerous 1,000-mile days, this was his first endurance rally.

Boyd Young, a restaurant owner from Atoka, Oklahoma, had been riding motorcycles since he was 13. He rode competi-

Marty Jones with his Kawasaki Voyager before the 1995 rally.
Although Marty competed in the 1993 Iron Butt, an accident in West
Virginia prevented him from finishing that event.

Harley riders included, *left to right:* Willie Thommes, Dennis Searcy,
Suzy Johnson, Phyllis Lang, Jesse Pereboom.

tively off-road until he tore his Achilles tendon in a motorcycle mishap in 1982. Now in his mid-thirties, he claims that between him and his 65-year-old father, more than 40 motorcycles have passed through their garage. He still owns a half-dozen of various makes.

Like me, Boyd had been reading about the Iron Butt Rally for years. This rally would be his first attempt at endurance riding.

Hooked on Harleys

Mike Kneebone claims that new riders most often ask if a Harley-Davidson has ever finished the Iron Butt. Despite the quality and reliability of recent Harley-Davidsons, many people, including motorcyclists who should know better, question the ability of a rider to finish such an ordeal on a Harley. The 1995 field of entrants included five Harleys, two ridden by women. Phyllis Lang, accompanied by her husband Fritz, on a Honda Silver Wing, hoped to be the first woman on a Harley to complete the Iron Butt.

The other woman riding a Harley was Mary Sue "Suzy" Johnson from Griffith, Indiana. When not participating in motorcycling events, she drives an 18-wheeler for Roadway Express. As a member of the Roadway Road Team, she attends fairs and festivals and travels to schools and civic organizations to improve the public image of trucking and to promote highway safety.

Suzy looks years younger than one would suppose after hearing of her six grown children and her grandchildren. She has no tattoos and doesn't look like anyone's preconception of a Harley-Davidson enthusiast. Like Phyllis Lang, Suzy arrived hoping to be the first woman to finish the rally on a Harley.

Contrary to the "outlaw" image of Harley riders, they are some of the most pleasant and interesting members of the motorcycling community. Jesse Pereboom, with long blonde hair that reaches his waist, and Dennis Searcy, with long black hair, mustache and tattooed arms, came closest to satisfying the stereotype of a Harley "biker."

Marty Jones (white shirt) and Ken Hatton (with his "Stealth Bike")
were the only riders mounted on Kawasakis.

Willie Thommes, usually accompanied by Dexter, his border collie, brought one of his Harley-Davidsons to the rally. The Harley that Willie rides with Dexter includes a small rug-covered platform between the handlebars. When Willie approaches the bike, Dexter usually beats him to it, placing himself squarely on the platform where he rides for as long as Willie wants to ride. When Willie stops at a restaurant along the highway and attaches Dexter's leash to the bike, Dexter is intent on protecting the bike from passers-by.

Willie elected to ride the Iron Butt solo, after deciding that locating dog-friendly motels would burn up too much time.

Big Dogs Don't Bite
The goal of most entrants is to finish. But top ranked "Big Dogs" from previous endurance events arrived with sights set much higher. They included previous Iron Butt Rally first place finishers Steve Attwood and Ron Major. Others included Harold Brooks, Jim Culp, Gary Eagan, Roy Eastwood, Eric Faires, Ken

Hatton, Eddie James, Marty Jones, Morris Kruemcke, Tom Loegering, Steve Losofsky, Eddie Metz, Gregg Smith, and Frank Taylor.

Eddie James was one of the most engaging riders of the group. Bob Higdon, a popular motorcycle journalist whose daily reports of the rally were published on the Internet, described Eddie as "a man who looks fast, even when he's walking." Eddie has become known for his constant riding companion, Lyle the Bear, a ragged teddy bear which accompanied him throughout the rally and on one occasion helped him avoid a traffic ticket. Of all the riders I met, he was the most intense—a young man obsessed with the desire to win. As I approached a group of riders where Eddie was holding court, he proclaimed his determination to place well in the rally. "It's my *destiny* to finish in the top five," he declared. "Even when I'm in bed with my girlfriend, I can't help thinking about how I can shave a few seconds off my fuel stops."

Eddie gained some attention when he finished at the end of the pack in 1993 after being hospitalized in Nevada for food poisoning. This year the rally would provide Eddie more attention and notoriety than he had anticipated. But it would come in a way that was unexpected. And unintended.

Ken Hatton, holder of the Guinness record for making it from New York to San Francisco in 41 hours and 17 minutes, was back again. Ken ran in the 1993 rally with his covert Kawasaki ZX-11 equipped with radar jammers, retractable antennas, police scanners, and other high-tech accoutrements. Ken had hopes of doing better than in 1993, when a broken gear sprocket forced him out.

"Big Dog" Tom Loegering had also returned, this year accompanied by his son, Tom Jr. Tom Sr., "The Hard Luck Kid of 1993," put in one of the most remarkable appearances in the previous rally, finishing seventh with his "dual sport" BMW R100GS in spite of numerous mechanical failures. Tom's first indication of trouble in 1993 occurred before the rally even began. Several hundred yards away from the starting line, the universal joint on his motorcycle broke. The owner of the BMW dealership in Fort Worth agreed to dismantle a new motorcycle to give Tom the parts he required to get started. Even with this help, Tom didn't get going until 90 minutes after the other riders had departed.

By the time he reached the first checkpoint in California, the motorcycle was running so badly Tom had to tear it down for a valve job. When he reached Spokane, he had to have the carburetors rebuilt, and when he reached Chicago he found that he had lost nearly all of his engine oil and that his charging system had failed. Bob Honemann from Bob's BMW in Chicago went to his aid, cannibalizing his own motorcycle to help get Tom going again. By this time, the other riders had a four-hour head start.

It wasn't until the fourth leg that Tom enjoyed the luxury of a ride undisturbed by mechanical trouble—and he had moved up to third place by the time he reached the Daytona checkpoint. But shortly after leaving Daytona, the charging system failed again. In spite of all this, Tom still finished the rally in seventh place. Fellow riders joked that Tom had replaced so many of the motorcycle's parts, he should be disqualified because he was no longer riding the same bike.

In his documentary of the rally, Bob Higdon wrote, "Having given the field yet *another* enormous head start, Loegering steamed forward and moved up from ninth place to seventh. There may never be an Iron Butt story as awesome as this. If the man doesn't get a standing ovation at the awards ceremony, life is truly more cruel than his own bike."

Frank Taylor, a previous winner of the Utah 1088 and second place finisher in the 1993 Iron Butt, was also entered. Frank has a reputation as one of the fastest endurance riders in the group. If I were a casting director searching for a lead actor for a movie about endurance riding, I would pick Frank. Unlike most riders, Frank *looks* like a man who would push off to touch the four corners of the U.S., and then some, in an 11-day motorcycle trip. With a solid build, square jaw, and thick mustache, he would do equally well in the role of tough cop or construction supervisor.

Frank is fortunate to have married a woman who loves motorcycling as much as he does. Jessica was introduced to the sport in 1991 when she and Frank were first dating. She was in

Fort Worth for the start and finish of the 1993 Iron Butt Rally to see Frank capture second place.

Jessica is a lot more than Frank's cheerleader. She rode "two-up" with Frank to compete in the 1995 Utah 1088. Together, they outscored every other rider, covering more miles and collecting the most points, only to be disqualified for returning to the finish line a few minutes late after being delayed by a traffic accident. The man who disqualified them had been the best man at their wedding: rallymaster Steve Chalmers.

Of all of the "Big Dogs" present this year, none was better-known in endurance riding circles than Ron Major from Temple City, California. I approached Ron as he was displaying a custom-made auxiliary fuel system to a group of riders. Ron won the Iron Butt Rally in 1991 but wrecked his motorcycle and was nearly killed in Gorham, Maine, during the 1993 rally. This year, he hoped to finish safely in the top ten without being ticketed for speeding. He intended to ride much more conservatively than he had in 1993.

Ron rides an average of 60,000 miles per year and has participated in more rallies than most hard-core endurance riding enthusiasts. He has a side business, Major Engineering, which develops accessories allowing a rider to convert a Honda ST1100 into an awesome Iron Butt machine. His products include a fully integrated auxiliary fuel system, heated seat, heated handlebar grips, and custom brackets for high-intensity driving lights. Ron is the recognized authority to whom other riders turn for advice about strengthening the ST1100.

Forum for Freshmen

Two pre-rally events were conducted the Monday before the rally: a meeting for novice riders and a rider's dinner. Gregg Smith, a veteran of three previous Iron Butt rallies, led the first. If he completed this rally, Gregg would hold the record for completing more Iron Butt Rallies than any other rider.

Gregg dispensed tips to the riders, emphasizing safety and caution. He discussed the importance of getting adequate sleep, recommending that riders check into a motel every night, even if only to get three or four hours of sleep. Steve Attwood, the winner of the rally in 1993, made a presentation on the importance of staying hydrated, particularly in the heat. He emphasized the importance of keeping leathers or Gore-Tex garments on, no matter how much heat the rider is encountering. I had purchased an Aerostich riding suit a few weeks before the rally. Because I didn't have experience wearing the Aerostich in the 100°F temperatures we were having, I had strapped it to the back of the motorcycle when I left home for Salt Lake City. After Steve's lecture, I promised myself that in the future I would wear the Aerostich, regardless of the temperature.

When Garve Nelson was introduced at the meeting, the riders rose to give him a standing ovation. At 71 years old, Garve was the oldest rider to ever complete the rally. A retired motorcycle dealer from San Leandro, California, Garve is an icon among endurance riding enthusiasts. He was winning speed trophies at the Bonneville Salt Flats before some of the younger riders were born. He was planning to run this rally on the second smallest bike entered, a 500cc Honda.

Distinguished Diners

Contestants, friends, wives, competitors from previous rallies, and other enthusiasts attended the riders' dinner. One of the most notable guests was Bob Higdon, a retired District of Columbia trial attorney and a director of the Iron Butt Association. He is past vice-president of the BMW Motorcycle Owners Association and a former member of the activist Motorcycle Riders Foundation. He writes a monthly column for *On the Level,* the magazine of the BMW Riders Association. In 1993, the American Motorcycle Association named him Road Rider of the Year for his work in helping to open Virginia's high-occupancy vehicle lanes to commuting motorcycle riders. He's also a regular contributor to *Rider, Motorcyclist, and Motorcycle Consumer News.*

Bob rose to deliver one of the "benedictions" that he often offers at pre-rally gatherings. He pointed out that normally priests or ministers deliver benedictions. He went on to suggest that priests can offer heaven and happiness but lawyers can promise only hell. This was good for a laugh.

I didn't learn until after the rally that Bob planned to publish daily accounts of our progress on the Internet. At the time, I wasn't on-line and didn't realize how many motorcyclists were into the world of e-mail and web-surfing.

England's Entry

Steve Attwood, who sat next to me at dinner, is an unassuming guy who makes you feel very comfortable, and also makes you feel fortunate to have the opportunity to learn of his travels. He isn't shy, but he isn't a braggart either. He had shipped his motorcycle to the U.S. from his home in England to participate in his second Iron Butt Rally. He won the 1993 event on a nondescript motorcycle—limping to the finish line on one cylinder, without the benefit of a laptop computer or radar detector, while riding on what to him was the wrong side of the road.

Several years earlier, Steve and his wife, Debra, spent two years on an around-the-world motorcycle tour, covering 56,000 miles and 22 countries. While they reserved their highest praise for the highway crossing the United States's western desert, they also had fond memories of New Zealand and Turkey—and a healthy respect for the difficult roads of India, where each of their 11 flat tires drew an audience.

Although most motorcycling accidents happen close to home, Steve seems to be at greater risk the farther he gets from England. He's crashed twice in France and once each in Greece, Yugoslavia, Egypt, and the U.S., all but the last with Debra, who usually bore the brunt of the impact. "We're still married, but she rides her own bike now," he quipped.

Despite these misfortunes, or maybe because of them, Steve's riding style is conservative. He counts on consistency and discipline, rather than raw speed.

Local Legend

By contrast, my other dinner partner, Gary Eagan, was one of the fastest riders entered. Gary, who lives in Salt Lake City, had just finished first in the Utah 1088. While doing so, he also set a new 24-hour mileage mark at 1,931 miles. He also won a new BMW motorcycle for raising the largest contributions for Pro-

Skip Ciccarelli (left) and Steve Attwood, the first place finisher of the 1993 Iron Butt Rally, were the only Moto Guzzi riders. Coincidentally, both men suffered the same fate and were unable to finish the rally. (Shown here with Attwood's bike.)

ject Hope. (Gary sold the motorcycle he won in the Utah 1088. He used the same motorcycle in the Iron Butt that he had used for the Utah 1088.)

Of all of the dedicated riders I have met, none takes endurance riding more seriously than Gary. Most of the riders have radar detectors. Gary has several, including one "shrink-wrapped" in plastic for use in the rain. Gary was also one of the few riders using a radar jammer to confound police radar.

Gary also puts great care into preparing himself for the demands of the contest: running 20 to 30 miles a week, using a stationary bike, and doing weight training and stretching exercises. He also did a lot of riding in the four months preceding the rally.

The Rallybastard and the Rules

Steve Chalmers led the dinner festivities. During his introductory speech, he admitted to earning the moniker "Rallybastard" as manager of the Utah 1088. He was such a stickler for the rules that during the most recent Utah 1088, he disqualified Frank Taylor, one of his closest friends.

Although Steve had explained the Iron Butt in his previous letters to the riders, he reviewed it again: At 4:00 p.m. the next day, one hour prior to the rally's start, "rally packets" would be distributed. These would contain a description of bonus opportunities for the leg between Salt Lake City and Spokane, the first checkpoint. The two-hour checkpoint window would open in Spokane at 3 p.m., Pacific time Wednesday, 23 hours after the start of the rally. Riders arriving during this two-hour period would earn a checkpoint bonus of 2,000 points. Although there would be no advantage for arriving early, riders would lose one point for every minute after 3 p.m. that they arrived.

At each checkpoint the rider would have to surrender evidence of having visited bonus locations. Depending on the bonus, proof of the visit could consist of a Polaroid picture taken at the location, a gasoline receipt, toll receipt, or some other acceptable tidbit. To ensure that the photo hadn't been taken before the start of the rally, the photo would have to include a particular object Steve would hand out at the dinner.

Immediately after the window closed at 5 p.m. in Spokane, the riders would receive rally packets for the second leg, which would end in San Diego on Friday September 1, 41 hours later, at the start of the Labor Day weekend. The third leg would terminate in Ft. Lauderdale, the fourth in Gorham, Maine, and the fifth back in Salt Lake City on September 9. Checkpoint bonuses and penalty points for being late would increase as the rally progressed.

Steve made it clear that he would enforce the rules "by the book." He suggested that top finishers might be required to take a drug test. Any of several deeds would result in a rider's disqualification, or worse. A rider who failed to assist an injured rider, he noted, would be well advised to skip post-rally festivities. This was not the same as helping a rider who had encountered mechanical problems or who had run out of fuel. It was perfectly acceptable to pass by a fellow rider whose tank was empty, but anyone who drove past an injured rider faced instant disqualification. Anyone who lost precious time by stopping to help, on the other hand, would be granted an extra time allowance.

We were also enjoined to treat checkpoint workers courteously, no matter how cranky sleep deprivation and long, hard miles had made us. After all, the checkpoint workers were volunteers.

Finally, Steve emphasized the importance of planning and strategy and cautioned the group against excessive speeding. "The Iron Butt isn't about trying to make it around the United States at 95 mph," he advised. "If you try that, you'll probably just get yourself arrested."

Storm Signals

After explaining the rules, Steve invited questions.

"There's hurricane activity going on off the coast of Florida right now," remarked a rider. "What should we do if there's a hurricane raging when we're due to be at the Ft. Lauderdale checkpoint?"

"The weather won't change anything," Steve replied. "I will guarantee you that someone will be there to check you in. It may not be the same people who we are currently planning to operate the checkpoint, but someone will be there. The Burger King checkpoint location may have been blown away, but someone *will* be waiting there where it stood."

The Atlantic Ocean hurricane season officially runs from June 1 to November 30, and the Iron Butt Rally takes place right in the middle of it. Steve didn't know it at the time, but the 1995 hurricane season was beginning to look as if it might be one of the stormiest in the last hundred years. For the last two months, things had been off and running in a nearly unbroken, often overlapping, succession of storms. The 1966 all-time record for the greatest number of storms during the month of July had been tied after the fourth storm, Erin, hit Florida's east coast and western panhandle, causing approximately $700 million in damage and six deaths. Tropical Storm Jerry, though not qualifying as a hurricane, had ended only days before. Hurricane Luis was heading for the Caribbean from Africa and threatened to smash into Florida too.

In exactly one week, riders were expected to arrive at the Ft. Lauderdale checkpoint. Several riders expressed apprehension about riding through heavy storms to get there. Their concerns about the weather were not unfounded.

Initial Introductions

Next, the riders introduced themselves and commented on their prior endurance riding experience and reasons for entering this event. As riders spoke, the wives and "significant others" who accompanied them introduced themselves too. Several encouraged riders to exercise caution, reminding them of the loved ones who awaited their safe return.

Martin Hildebrandt told us how, as his interest in riding greater and greater distances grew, he found his circle of riding companions becoming smaller and smaller. He wanted to ride the Iron Butt with riders who shared his appetite for devouring incredible distances.

One rider quoted Helen Keller's description of life as a daring adventure. The quotation has always been a favorite of mine, and helps explain how these riders justify the risks to which they willingly expose themselves:

"Security is mostly a superstition. It does not exist in nature, nor do the children of humankind as a whole experience it. Avoiding danger is no safer in the long run than outright exposure. Life is either a daring adventure, or it is nothing at all."

Springing a Surprise

Steve Chalmers added to the adventure by announcing a surprise bonus: 3,000 points for visiting all 48 contiguous states. Some riders, like me, thought this was either flatly impossible or, at best, a distraction from the goal of collecting regular bonus points. Other riders, though, decided to attempt the 48-state feat, even though they had no idea whether it was worth the potential loss of other bonus opportunities.

Morris Kruemcke had anticipated such a bonus opportunity before arriving in Salt Lake City and had already decided to go for it if it was offered.

Marty Jones, on the other hand, said, "Now I can relax. Someone is going to do 48 states and it won't be me. I can't win, but I'm going to shoot for the top ten."

Martin Hildebrandt was sitting with Leonard Aron, an attorney from Ventura, California who was planning to ride an antique Indian Chief. Leonard was another CISsie whom Martin had met in cyberspace before he came to the United States. He had sent Martin a collection of AAA maps as backup to his electronic gadgetry.

"Sucker move," Leonard advised, referring to the surprise bonus. "That's one of Chalmers's damn traps."

Martin decided that, as an American, Leonard must know what was possible and what wasn't. He decided to forgo the 48-state challenge.

At the conclusion of the dinner, Chalmers issued the contestants small pink golf towels with their rider numbers. The towel was to appear in photographs taken by the rider at bonus locations to prove that the stop had been made. Chalmers cautioned riders that if they lost their towels, they could no longer claim bonus stops requiring photographs. Riders then signed a T-shirt that would be awarded to the winner.

Final Fine Tuning

After a good night's sleep, most riders spent Tuesday morning talking to friends and making final adjustments to their motorcycles and equipment. I arranged to keep my motel room until 5:00 p.m., the start of the rally. I wanted to take an after-

September 1995						
Mon	Tue	Wed	Thur	Fri	Sat	Sun
28	29	30	31	1	2	3
4	5	6	7	8	9	10
11	12	13	14	15	16	17
18	19	20	21	22	23	24
25	26	27	28	29	30	

noon nap and have a comfortable place to spread my maps and plan the first leg of the rally.

Brian Bush's video team wanted an opportunity to interview each rider. When I arrived in the parking lot for my interview, the crew was filming Eddie James, who was sitting on his motorcycle, discussing what it was like to undertake such a formidable task. The crew wanted plenty of footage of the riders likely to finish well. Considering Eddie's prior endurance riding experience, the film crew thought he was likely to finish near the top.

Later in the afternoon, I joined a small crowd of riders who surrounded Eddie while he worked on the recently fried wiring of his radio. His BMW was a sport tourer class with no facility for installation of a factory radio. He had rigged-up an after-market unit inside a tank bag and was now faced with last-minute repairs to get the bike running again. Eddie was frantic. Like the other riders, he had been looking forward to this rally for two years. Now, mere hours before the event was to begin, he wasn't certain that his motorcycle was going to be working.

Although Eddie's panicked state contrasted with that of the other riders, he wasn't the only rider who was glancing frequently at his watch. Several riders tried to lessen their anxiety by visiting local motorcycle shops or by taking short rides around the city. Others spread themselves out on the grass surrounding the parking lot and studied maps or napped.

After a few hours spent rebuilding the wiring, Eddie once again had his radio working and his motorcycle running.

Chalmers offered to synchronize clocks to insure that we would know the exact time of the rally clocks at the checkpoint locations. I had just finished packing my motorcycle, except for the Aerostich, maps, and helmet that were still in my motel room. "How important could a minute or two be, considering that we're about to start an 11-day rally?" I thought. I considered this a little melodramatic and chose instead to return to my room to study the maps of the area. Days later, while attempting to choose between missing a checkpoint or running out of gas, I would regret my cavalier attitude.

Eddie James being interviewed before the rally.

As 4:00 p.m. drew nearer, I made final preparations. During the previous months, I had augmented my equipment with extras necessary for the coming challenge. These included a portable water tank that I wore on my back, with a drinking tube I could use while wearing my helmet. I filled the bag with bottled water.

I inserted my contact lenses for the first time since leaving Plano. Wearing eyeglasses for the last several days had given my eyes a rest so that I could use the contact lenses for a longer period during the rally. I preferred them to eyeglasses for convenience and better vision.

"As these long rallies grind on and on, simple tasks get real annoying," Morris Kruemcke had explained to me. "You have to keep things as simple as possible or you'll drive yourself even more crazy than you were when you started the blasted thing."

I'd learned the wisdom of his words as a result of my 1,300 mile warm-up ride to Salt Lake City. Dealing with eyeglasses had been a nuisance. But I wasn't sure how the contacts would hold up on an 11-day ride.

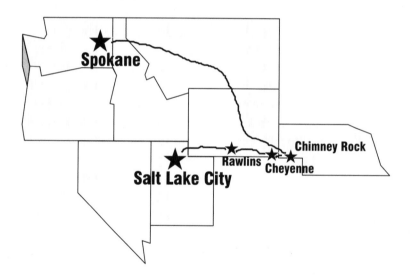

Leg 1 – Salt Lake City to Spokane, Author's Route

3

Salt Lake City to Spokane

720 Miles - 23 Hours

Countdown to Commencement

I returned to the parking lot at 4:00 p.m. to receive my first list of bonuses. The first leg would be an overnight ride to Spokane, departing Salt Lake City at 5:00 p.m. Riders had to travel a minimum of 720 miles in 23 hours. But a rider wouldn't be competitive if he elected to do only this easy base ride.

The package contained directions to Jim Plunkett's Tyre and Supply, the motorcycle shop that served as the Spokane checkpoint location. The package also included emergency phone numbers (to be used in the event of an accident or delay in reaching the checkpoint during the designated two-hour window) and the penalties for being late.

Riders would try to arrive by 3:00 p.m. when the checkpoint opened in Spokane. Riders would lose one point for each minute they were late; if a rider failed to arrive by 5:00 p.m., he would be "time barred" and suffer a penalty of 2,000 points, plus all the points earned for the leg—enough to eliminate him as a serious competitor. The rider would also be unable to earn bonus points for the following leg and would have to make all remaining checkpoints in the allotted time to qualify as a finisher.

The package also contained a fuel log for recording the time and odometer reading at each fuel stop. Although it wasn't mandatory to maintain a fuel log, riders could earn additional points for doing so.

My maps of the western United States still covered the floor when I returned to my room, rally packet in hand, to plot my route for the first leg. I studied the alternatives. I discounted the Alaska bonus immediately. Alaska, like several other bonuses that would be dangled before us during the next ten days, would be impossible to make within the allotted time. No one bit on it.

Two other tempting bonuses were located close together: the Dinosaur National Monument near Vernal, Utah, and the gas purchase from any gasoline station in Vernal. Gas was available 24 hours a day, but the Dinosaur National Monument was only open until 7:00 p.m., and it was virtually impossible to ride the 180 miles from Salt Lake City to Vernal in the two hours before closing time.

Picking Points to Pursue

Selecting a route for the first leg was challenging for Martin Hildebrandt, who hadn't yet spent his first week in the United States and hadn't learned to use the AAA maps that Leonard Aron had sent him. "I'll have no chance to find all of these locations on my maps in any reasonable time," he thought. "My computer doesn't know most of the places, and paper maps are useless to me. Every moment that I need to find locations that I will never travel to will be reduced from my available riding time. This is hopeless."

Martin decided to go for the 48-state bonus instead. He knew it was probably impossible, but it was better than enduring the frustration of trying to find all the obscure bonus locations. Besides, he decided, he could always give up the quest if it became obvious he couldn't do it. He was determined to finish, at least.

I reviewed the bonus opportunities and decided to attempt the toughest, highest value bonuses (except, of course, Alaska). This required riding from Salt Lake to Chimney Rock Historic Site in southwestern Nebraska, with stops in Rawlins and Cheyenne, Wyoming. I didn't expect it to be easy, but I thought I could do it.

As I was mounting up, fastening my helmet strap, and preparing to don my gloves, Mike Kneebone approached. "Where have you decided to go? Do you mind if I ask?"

"Think I'll go for the three big ones out east," I replied.

Mike shook his head as if to say, "Foolish fellow." "You'll burn yourself out, biting off so much on the first day," he told me.

Because the rally was about to start and I had already mentally committed to the long trek east, I decided to ignore Mike's admonition and go for it. But I felt uneasy as I reflected on Ardys Kellerman's and Morris Kruemcke's experiences two years before.

The rally that year started in Ft. Worth with the first checkpoint in Los Angeles. Any rider who started the rally by heading east, to Louisiana, could snatch a huge bonus, but Mike encouraged riders to ignore it.

Ardys and Morris decided to go for it anyway. After racking up 2,224 miles on her way to Los Angeles via Louisiana, Ardys was in second place but paid a high price in fatigue. She was time-barred at the next checkpoint in Spokane, lost 4,000 points as a result, and wound up finishing the rally ahead of only one other rider. But her next-to-last finish couldn't be blamed entirely on her ambitious bonus choice. Several weeks after the 1993 rally, she revealed she had ridden while fighting a severe case of Lyme disease and had been under treatment for a thyroid condition as well.

Morris, the only other rider to snatch the "bayou bonuses," had accumulated 2,259 miles and was in first place when he reached Los Angeles. He also finished the rally at the end of the pack, ahead of only Ardys and two others. This year, Ardys was focused on finishing and decided to just ride the checkpoints. But Morris was here to win.

Leaving the Line

I was the fifth or sixth rider of 55 to leave the starting line at the motel parking lot. I have to confess to being choked up as I realized the rally was beginning and I was participating. For me, the moment couldn't have been more emotional if the rally was the central event of the Olympics and the world was witnessing my departure.

During the first hour, I questioned whether I belonged out here with these guys. It was a question that had occurred to me often in the years leading up to this event. The rally attracts top riders from all over the country. I wondered if my performance during the next 11 days would betray me as an impostor. Was I a "wannabe," a Walter Mitty who, so far, had only managed to horn my way into this event with a $650 outfit and a $17,000 motorcycle? Aren't the lack of an auxiliary fuel tank and driving lights dead give-aways?

Impostor or not, I was having a ball, doing what I had waited so long to do.

At first I went east on I-80, in sight of several other riders who started off in the same direction. We climbed over the Wasatch Range of the Rocky Mountains, descended through Echo, and continued through the Echo Canyon on our way to the Wyoming border. Entering Wyoming, we crossed the old Oregon Trail near Ft. Bridger, where Brigham Young's advance party turned southwest and eventually came to the Great Salt Lake.

We continued to one of the major tourist oases in the region, Little America. I thought it interesting that this major stopping point was so close to the trail used a few centuries ago by pioneers on their way west. Large billboards every few miles along the highway invited today's travelers to stop for fuel, food, and rest.

"Steak-out your claim," read one, with a 20-foot-high photograph of an enticing steak dinner.

"Get the big picture," proclaimed another, with a subtitle promising potential guests a large-screen TV.

Although the Iron Butt doesn't provide time for steak dinners, TV, or traditional sight-seeing, the scenery is captivating. I was already fascinated by the unusual rock formations in southwestern Wyoming. In many places, the formations mutated from one shade of brown to another, acquiring a deep green hue near the peaks.

I took my first fuel stop in Little America, about 160 miles from Salt Lake. I was the first in the group to stop, the only one in that group without an auxiliary fuel supply. After refueling, I removed a small notebook that I had packed and recorded a few short lines. The Iron Butt was an important event in my life and I wanted to reflect on it in the future. There wasn't much time for writing during the rally, though—the best I was able to do was to scribble an occasional thought. At the time, I had no intention of publishing anything. My purpose was merely to preserve my memories.

Promontory Point Points

I quickly mounted the bike and continued east through Green River and Rock Springs on the way to Rawlins and Cheyenne. Even before I stopped at Little America, riders with less ambitious first-day objectives had already bagged their first 21 bonus points at Promontory Point in northern Utah. The "Golden Spike" was hammered into the earth at this location in 1869 to unite the Union Pacific and Central Pacific railroads, creating the nation's first transcontinental railroad.

Karol Patzer arrived at the Golden Spike Historical Site to find Ardys Kellerman, Gregg Smith, and Jim Culp already there. Karol, the mileage contest coordinator for the BMW Motorcycle Owners of America, had equipped her motorcycle with an expanded capacity fuel tank. The motorcycle now held eight gallons of fuel and allowed her to ride nearly 300 miles between stops. But Karol was unaccustomed to the weight of the additional three gallons when she placed it on the sidestand in an area that caused it to lean more than usual. The additional fuel added less than 20 pounds to the weight of the motorcycle, but all of the weight was above the center of gravity. Fortunately for Karol, Jim was available to help get her 550-pound motorcycle upright. She was more cautious when she parked the motorcycle during the next ten days.

Karol's motorcycle was heavy compared to Ed Otto's Helix, but wasn't the largest or heaviest motorcycle in the rally. Her three-cylinder K75S weighed about half that of Jim's fully loaded, six-cylinder Gold Wing. Gold Wings are so heavy that, unlike other motorcycles used in the rally, many of them include a reverse gear so the rider can extricate the motorcycle from a downward-sloping parking space.

The beginning hours of the rally for Tom Loegering were as serene as the first hours of his 1993 ride were frenzied. He too chose a relatively leisurely route to Spokane and made his first bonus stop at Promontory Point. Although he decided to pursue the 3,000-point bonus for visiting all 48 states, he began his ride at a relaxed pace. He and his son met on the way to Spokane, shared a motel room, and got a good night's sleep.

Near Table Rock, I crossed the Continental Divide, which directs the flow of the nation's rainfall to either the Atlantic or Pacific shores. I rode parallel to the Divide almost all the way to Rawlins. The Divide headed south for the Colorado Rockies. I continued east.

Promontory Point Pass

As I was approaching Rawlins, Suzy Johnson was considering whether to proceed with her plan to pick up the 21-point Golden Spike bonus. Earlier, while other riders were stopping to collect this relatively easy bonus, Suzy was bagging 86 points by visiting a similar attraction to the south: the Railroad Museum in Helper, Utah. Now, in the vicinity of the Golden Spike bonus, darkness had fallen and she was quickly approaching the turn-off to the bonus location.

"It's a gravel road and at this time of night there will be plenty of rattlesnakes all over it," an attendant at a nearby gasoline station had recently advised. "Besides, it's dark out there. Be real careful."

After the warning, Suzy headed for the monument at Prom-ontory Point anyway. But as she approached the dark gravel road and had to make the "go/no go" decision, she was overcome with apprehension and opted for "no go." Suzy's no wimp, but she doesn't like snakes. Her decision was validated when she later learned from Jerry Clemmons that he had seen a rattle-snake on the road when he was exiting the area earlier in the evening.

Although this was Suzy's first motorcycle endurance rally, the event wasn't her first motor vehicle competition. She has won a number of truck competitions in which she demonstrated her proficiency in handling semis. This was Suzy's first Iron Butt only because rallymaster Jan Cutler rejected her application in 1991. Jan didn't believe that Suzy had enough riding experience. If she became injured during the rally, it would be difficult to explain why he had believed she was qualified to participate. Beginning in 1993, however, eligibility was based strictly on a drawing. Suzy tried to enter again, calling Mike Kneebone for registration information. The list had already been filled, but she was in line to participate in 1995.

By the time I was entering Rawlins, Bob Higdon was already responding to one of his first e-mail messages about the rally.

Bob,

What chance do you give the fellow who is riding the Helix?

Charlie

Tue Aug 29, 1995 11:50 EDT

Charlie:

Ed Otto, on a 250cc Honda Helix scooter, is a good rider with some solid credentials. I don't think that will be enough. He's not going for a win. He just wants to ride checkpoint to checkpoint.

Eddie's finished the Iron Butt Rally before. It won't happen this time.

Bob Higdon

I didn't see other riders again until I stopped for fuel in Rawlins. After taking a picture of my towel draped over the visitor sign at the old prison building, I signed the photograph and recorded the time and odometer reading on the back. I placed the photograph into a small vinyl bank deposit bag and proceeded to my next bonus selection, a statue of Abraham Lincoln near Cheyenne. This was going to be great fun!

Great fun, except for the aggravating routine that I would have to perform at each stop. Stop the bike, turn off the engine, dismount, remove gloves, remove helmet, get towel and camera out of storage, place towel at the bonus location, snap the picture, record odometer mileage and time on log sheets and on the back of the photograph, and reverse the process.

The routine would be no less annoying when I stopped for gas. Instead of removing the camera and towel for a photograph, I would have to lift the motorcycle onto the centerstand, remove the tank bag to get access to the fuel tank, and refuel the motorcycle. Whenever I removed my helmet, one or both of my earplugs would fall out, requiring that I remove another from the tank bag, shape it to my ear, and insert it. Considering the dozen photos and 86 fuel stops that I would make, I would repeat the tedious routine a hundred times during the next week and a half.

Conferring with Confederates

I arrived at the statue of Abraham Lincoln and took the picture as Rick Shrader and Gary Eagan were arriving. Gary reported that he had just seen a rider being ticketed by a Wyoming State Trooper. "If I get one more ticket, I'll lose my license for a while," Rick confessed.

We discussed the bonus in Chimney Rock, another 160 miles in the opposite direction from our Spokane destination. I suspected that Gary was trying to psyche us out of attempting Chimney Rock, as he emphasized that the first leg total would amount to more than 1,600 miles. My calculations indicated I would have to ride less than 1,500 miles. Was I already succumbing to the lure? Was I pursuing the distant Nebraska bonus like a trout following the fisherman's fly?

"Be a damn shame to not do it after coming this far," noted Rick. I agreed and decided to steam ahead, leaving my two comrades in the parking lot to finish the discussion.

As I was approaching Cheyenne, I stopped again for gas. Gary and Rick flew past on their way to Nebraska. As I was refueling, I remembered the summer of 1991, when my son David and I stopped in Cheyenne on our way home from the Grand Tetons and Yellowstone in northwestern Wyoming. Nature was putting on a spectacular light show in the form of a thunderstorm, and was dumping rain all over us. I had been through Cheyenne several other times, but this was the first time I could remember passing through without the ride being accompanied by thunder and lightning.

David and I had checked into a motel for the night and departed Cheyenne at daylight, planning to spend the next night in Amarillo, Texas. After a hearty dinner David suggested that we continue, rather than stop for the night. We had already traveled more than 500 miles and the remainder of the trip made more than 900 miles for the day. We arrived home at 3 a.m. Many riders, after enduring 1,000 miles in a day, have no desire ever to willingly subject themselves to such an ordeal again. At the time I wouldn't have believed I could complete another ten such days consecutively.

Trooper's Target

It was after midnight on Wednesday morning at Kimball, Nebraska, when I left the relative safety of the interstate highway system for the first time since Salt Lake City. I shifted through the gears of the motorcycle as I left the exit ramp, concentrating on shifting mental gears as well. I wanted to be alert to the additional hazards of two-way traffic and intersections.

I soon saw the unmistakable flashing lights of a State Police cruiser and hoped it didn't mean a rider had been stopped. As I feared, Rick Shrader was parked in front of the cruiser as the officer wrote a ticket. I felt sorry for him as I remembered his recent words about his license not being able to withstand the weight of another ticket.

September 1995						
Mon	Tue	Wed	Thur	Fri	Sat	Sun
28	29	30	31	1	2	3
4	5	6	7	8	9	10
11	12	13	14	15	16	17
18	19	20	21	22	23	24
25	26	27	28	29	30	

Rick and the trooper had been heading toward each other. Rick's motorcycle was equipped with a radar jammer that confused the trooper's radar. But as the vehicles passed each other, Rick's speed was captured by the officer's *rear-facing* radar. The trooper executed the classic U-turn and pulled Rick over.

Gary had been riding a little ahead of Rick and was the unsuspecting recipient of a dose of good luck. Gary had reached for an energy bar, opening the wrapper with his teeth, which necessitated slowing the motorcycle. He would otherwise have taken the hit rather than Rick.

Several miles before I reached Chimney Rock, I saw Gary returning from that direction. I didn't see him again until Spokane. I didn't know it at the time, but I would be following on Gary's heels for much of the coming week. Whenever I stopped to collect a large bonus, Gary would already have been there. I developed a great deal of respect for his solid riding ability.

Elusive Entrance

I began following tourist signs to the Chimney Rock Historic Site and turned onto a small side road, expecting to arrive at the entrance to the visitor center. I soon found myself on gravel, surrounded by high shrubbery, and in total darkness at a dead-end. I realized that I should have brought a quality flashlight. I started down a dirt road, nearly dropping the motorcycle several times in deep, soft sand. After deciding that the rally wouldn't require street bikes to deal with off-road conditions, I carefully turned around and returned to pavement.

Rick Shrader arrived and also had difficulty finding the visitor center. We had a brief discussion about the probable location of the elusive bonus. I told him that I had started down the dirt road but doubted the rally required negotiation of such a trail.

Rick had no such reservations. "Guess I'll have to rely on my old dirt-biking experience," he chuckled, as he headed down the trail in a cloud of dust. I knew that Rick owns a "racing hack"—a Kawasaki with a sidecar—but I wasn't aware that his background included off-road work too.

I backtracked to where I'd spotted the last sign to the historic site. I had never been to Chimney Rock but decided that the name of the attraction must refer to a prominent geological monument of some sort. It was very dark, but as I studied the horizon I finally was able to identify the craggy silhouette of the site's namesake. I headed in the direction of the monument and located the visitor center, cloaked in near-total darkness by the road. I sounded my horn to alert Rick, who was out of earshot. I watched his tail lights disappear into the darkness.

I later learned that Chimney Rock is the most famous landmark on the Oregon Trail and is mentioned in 95 percent of the pioneers' diaries. If I had arrived several hours earlier, I would have had no difficulty in locating the monolith, as it's illuminated after dark, though not 24 hours a day.

I parked the motorcycle, removed my helmet and gloves, and took the camera from the tour pack. I placed the towel on the sign and took the picture. After logging the time and odometer reading, and signing and placing the photograph in an envelope, I reversed the process. While replacing the camera in the tour pack, I studied the atlas to reconfirm my route for the trip to Spokane. I replaced my helmet and gloves and began to leave the parking lot.

From the corner of my eye, I noticed my pink rider towel, still hanging on the visitor sign.

"This is day one and it's only been 12 hours since I had a nap. I shouldn't be that tired yet," I thought. "What will happen a week from now when I've banged out eight or ten thousand miles?"

I retrieved the towel and committed to add this item to my mental checklist after each stop—DON'T LEAVE THE TOWEL. I remembered Steve Chalmers's admonition as he distributed the towels: "Lose your towel and you won't be able to collect additional photo bonuses."

I rode through Wyoming via Scottsbluff, Douglas, Casper, and Buffalo. From Chimney Rock to Casper, my route coincided exactly with the old Oregon Trail, heading west. At Casper, I-25 and the trail diverge, with the Interstate heading north to Buffalo, where it joins I-90. I headed for Buffalo.

Friends have often asked how I can stand hour after hour of silence and solitude on such rides. I'm almost never bored while riding at night. Somehow, a special kind of relaxation comes with slicing through the night air on a good road in good weather, with only the sound of the engine's exhaust and the tires against the road, the bike's headlight illuminating the way ahead. I reflected on how much I love this type of riding as I made my way through my initial evening of the Iron Butt, toward the first checkpoint in Spokane. I felt very, very fortunate to be there.

Seized by Sand

During my ride through Montana, several riders were encountering serious problems with a construction area on the direct route to Spokane. About five hours out of Salt Lake City, Hank Rowland passed Horst Haak, and Horst decided to keep pace with Hank. After an hour or so, Horst noticed construction warning signs advising a maximum safe speed of 35 mph. He slowed, but Hank wasn't slowing down.

A few moments later Hank hit soft sand and gravel, lost control of the motorcycle, and fell. He heard the sound of an eighteen-wheeler applying the brakes behind him. All he could think was, "Damn! Two years of total preoccupation with this ride and I'm out of it before I even get started!"

Horst noticed a cloud of dust when Hank went down, then saw that his motorcycle was turned around with the headlight shining at Horst as he worked to keep his own bike from going over in the loose gravel and sand. When Horst stopped, the truck driver was already struggling to help Hank raise the motorcycle. It required all three of them to get the half-ton bike upright. Although the motorcycle was still operable, the engine guard was separated from the frame and the left saddlebag had been torn from the bike. Hank decided to delay repairs until he reached Spokane.

Willie Thommes, who had been a short distance ahead of Hank, had been one of the first riders to hit the deep gravel and nearly lost control of his motorcycle. Glancing in his rear-view mirrors, he saw a cloud of dust behind him as he struggled to slow the motorcycle without dropping it. He didn't learn of Hank's mishap until he reached Spokane.

The same hazard nearly cost Charles Elberfeld a dropped bike as he negotiated the construction area a few minutes later. After stopping to talk to the other riders, Charles stalled his motorcycle when he tried to take off with the bike still in third gear. As he couldn't remember having done that in the last 20 years, he presumed that he was a bit nervous.

For Charles, the rally was already presenting some tough challenges. After he left the construction area, he checked into a motel, where he suffered a bout of dry heaves. It subsided after he ate some snacks, so he set his alarm for 3:30 a.m. and went to sleep.

I stopped in Scottsbluff, the location of another prominent natural landmark used by the pioneers more than 100 years ago. It was about 2:30 a.m. when I began looking for an all-night gasoline station. There was only one 24-hour station in town, and it wasn't on the main road. As I stopped at an all-night diner to ask for directions, I began to appreciate the difference an auxiliary tank would have made. I didn't know it at the time, but at least one rider was already running out of gas on this rally and experienced a mini-adventure in finding more.

Stranded So Soon?
Martin Hildebrandt stopped in Downey, Idaho, for gasoline. After filling the motorcycle he entered the station to pay for his purchase.

"I need a dated receipt, Ma'am," Martin informed the young girl behind the counter.

"You're the crazy German, aren't you?" she asked. The girl told Martin that Leonard Aron stopped for fuel earlier and told her all about the rally and about his friend, the rider from Germany.

"With my foreign motorcycle, the glowing plasma display behind the windscreen, my foreign clothes and my German accent, I apparently put some flavor into her life," Martin wrote after the rally. "She wanted to pull me into a conversation. She seemed to be ready to hop on the back of the motorcycle and vanish into the night with me."

Martin continued through Montana toward Spokane, thinking about all of the people in the world who would never make such a trip. He was feeling very happy and very privileged. Finish or not, he knew this would be the trip of a lifetime.

As he continued through the night, he set Pan-Galactica to high resolution and received a warning about curves in the interstate at least 100 yards in advance. He marveled at being on the main north-south artery in a state the size of Germany without seeing another vehicle for 15 minutes. His thoughts were interrupted by the sight of his friend Leonard Aron pushing the old Indian Chief along the shoulder of the highway.

"The poor guy misjudged the old lady's thirst and was stranded in the middle of nowhere with no fuel," Martin reported. "He was embarrassed and too proud to ask for help. He knew that time that I spend for him takes time from my personal schedule. He tried to send me away, but leaving someone in the middle of Montana to make him fail the first leg of the run of his lifetime is nothing I would do to my worst enemy."

Martin removed one of his tie downs and attached it to the rear of his motorcycle and to the Indian's engine guard. He then towed the Indian at a comfortable 60 mph clip.

Things worked fine until the tow line broke as the motorcycles were exiting the highway for a gasoline station. Leonard once again encouraged Martin to proceed without him. Martin knotted the ends of the tow line together and began pulling the Indian again.

It was 2:00 a.m. and the only station in town was closed. But the riders got lucky, or so they thought when they found the owner of the gasoline station among the last three patrons of the only open bar in town. Martin's German accent helped persuade the owner to open the station to sell Leonard the needed fuel. But the only octane available was 85, and Leonard claimed that the Indian wouldn't run on it. Again refusing to be sent away, Martin continued towing the Indian until they found suitable fuel in Dillon, Montana.

Leonard had given Martin an Indian polo shirt in Salt Lake City. Martin now felt that he had earned it. After warming up in the station, Martin took off again for Spokane, leaving Leonard standing there, smiling, his hands full of junk food.

Empty So Early?

Meanwhile, I was in north-central Wyoming, about midway between the Black Hills of South Dakota and Yellowstone National Park, when I began having my own gas worries. As I approached Buffalo at the intersection of I-90 and I-25, the fuel gauge was indicating empty. I had never run out of fuel with this motorcycle, but I had with my older K100RS. Before running completely dry, the fuel injection system on the RS provided a warning. The motorcycle began to lurch. Reducing speed would alleviate the situation for a short time. The motorcycle would begin lurching again, requiring another reduction in speed. The only time I ran out of fuel with that bike, I was traveling less than 20 mph.

I expected the same behavior from the LT. The warning never came, so I assumed the bike had plenty of fuel. I was wrong. Considering how much fuel I was able to put into the tank when I arrived in Buffalo, I couldn't have gone another ten miles.

By the time I crossed into Montana, it was daylight. I continued via Crow Agency, Big Timber, Butte, and Missoula, and finally entered Idaho near Coeur d'Alene. I periodically calculated the time and distance remaining to Spokane. I wanted to avoid a screw-up this early in the rally, especially after being warned by Mike Kneebone. I again questioned if I had bitten off more than I could chew, which Mike claims is the major reason that some riders either don't finish the rally or don't finish well.

I always enjoy riding through Wyoming and Montana. The roads are great and the State Police are few and far between. The first leg provided no close encounters, except when a coyote darted across my path while I was doing over 80 mph. The animal was running at full speed and seemed as startled as I as it crossed within a few feet of my front tire.

Passing Problems

Lolo, Montana, was a popular bonus location for the first leg. Karol Patzer, murf, Greg Smith, Eddie James, Charles Elberfeld, Hank Rowland, Horst Haak, Tom Loegering, and a number of other riders visited this easy first leg bonus. On leaving Lolo, Hank Rowland and Horst Haak became ensnared in a traffic jam in the middle of town. Not seeing traffic coming from the other direction, Hank hauled on past all the stalled cars until he came upon a house in the middle of the road. A fair-sized bungalow was being moved down the center of the street.

The bungalow sat on a large flatbed, followed by a ratty old dump truck. The trucks were creeping at a snail's pace. Eager to get to Spokane in time to fix his broken engine guard and have time for a nap, Hank slithered to the front of the line to pass the procession.

When the grizzled old coot driving the dump truck saw Hank trying to cut in front of all the traffic, he swerved his truck in Hank's direction. The truck was moving slowly enough to provide Hank with time to jump up on the sidewalk, where he passed the house and continued to Spokane. Horst, exhibiting a more conservative riding style, caught up with Hank a few miles down the road.

Two slow-moving riders were having a passing problem of a different sort. They couldn't pass anything. Ed Otto and Bob Honemann, who was riding a 35-year-old BMW R60/2, had decided to ride together and were attempting to climb over the Bitterroot Range between Salt Lake City and Spokane at something less than 40 mph. Bob, a motorcycle shop owner from Chicago, was riding the vintage bike without a fairing or windshield and probably couldn't expect to do much more than Ed's Helix. He decided to take advantage of the Helix's powerful quartz headlight to help him see at night.

Ed had invested more than a year in planning for this rally but overlooked testing the Helix at the high altitudes that comprised a lot of the route in the western United States. He was now finding that the heavily loaded Helix could barely manage 40 mph while climbing 6 percent uphill grades into a head wind at an altitude of 4,000 feet.

"I expected power to be down, but never in my wildest dreams did I expect this loss of acceleration and top speed at altitude," Ed wrote in an article for *Motorcycle Consumer News* after the rally. "I had to formulate a new game plan. My plans of averaging 60 mph were out the window. I would now have to give up my one Iron Butt luxury: a motel room for a three-hour catnap every night. I would also learn a new skill: the art of drafting large semis and eating diesel fumes."

Spokane Sojourn

I passed through Coeur d'Alene a little past 3:00 p.m. as the window was opening in Spokane. Once again, I became worried about running out of gas. I knew I was already losing one point for each minute that I delayed my arrival in Spokane, but I didn't want to chance running out of gas and losing even more points. Worse, I would risk being time-barred. I stopped in Post Falls to refuel just before crossing the state line into Washington.

I arrived in Spokane a little over an hour after the window opened, losing enough points to put me in third place behind Gary Eagan and Rick Shrader. I learned that only the three of us rode the long ride to Nebraska. We collected the same bonuses, but I was the latest getting to the checkpoint, arriving four minutes after Rick. Although third place was a remarkable achievement for an "impostor," I was reluctant to abandon my self-imposed status, as this was only the first leg. Mike Kneebone had predicted that I would fade into obscurity.

I called Barb from the parking lot on my cellular phone. This was the first occasion I had to use the phone on the trip. I brought the phone on the rally in anticipation of a queue of riders waiting to use phones at the checkpoints.

Rick Shrader approached and asked how many miles I had covered in the 24 hours since leaving Salt Lake City. When I told him that my odometer indicated 1,425 miles, he stated that he had ridden about ten miles more. This distance represented "personal bests" for both of us. Unlike other riders, Rick, Gary, and I had gotten no sleep during this first leg.

We learned that Skip Ciccarelli had hit a deer and could not make it to the checkpoint. He needed parts for his motorcycle and hoped to find them and effect repairs in time to make San Diego.

Since Martin Hildebrandt had decided to not chase any bonuses for the first leg, he arrived refreshed, having slept a full eight hours in Haugan, Montana, only 100 miles from Spokane. All he had to turn in to Jim Plunkett were his state sign photographs.

"I can't see the towel in this picture," said Plunkett, an Iron Butt Rally veteran himself, as he examined the photograph of Martin's motorcycle pushed beneath the "Welcome to Wyoming" sign.

"What towel?" asked Martin.

"The towel that you were told to put in every picture to prove that you hadn't done the shot some time before the rally," responded Plunkett.

Martin felt stupid enough to cry. He hadn't fully understood the instructions about the towel and thought that it was required only at bonus locations. He had invested a lot of time in riding to the Wyoming border to capture the photograph, and now found that it was worthless. His first attempt to gather points had failed and he wouldn't have much of an opportunity to correct the mistake.

The Rallybastard Relents

Plunkett called Steve Chalmers to petition for an exception. Knowing of Steve's "Rallybastard" moniker, he didn't expect much sympathy.

"I'll accept it *this one time only* because you suffer the disadvantage of understanding the rules in a second language," Steve told him. "You really should try to get another shot on the way back."

Martin was relieved, but not happy. "I suppose I'm not as professional as I thought," he muttered to himself as he headed for the refreshments Plunkett's shop provided for the riders. His standing in Spokane was number 26, behind Leonard Aron who managed one minor bonus, even with his "out of fuel" delay.

It surprised me to learn that Eddie James declined the Chimney Rock bonus. We passed each other several times between Salt Lake City and Rawlins, and I assumed we were heading for the same destination. Eddie collected the bonuses for the old prison in Rawlins and for the statue of Lincoln near Cheyenne, then turned toward Spokane.

"It's smart not to attempt too much too early," Eddie remarked. "At least, that's what conventional wisdom says." Considering his "whistling in the dark" tone, I didn't think Eddie was happy with his decision.

During the final hours of my ride to Spokane, my head began to itch. Although I had experienced the problem from time to time in the past, it was usually at the end of a ride, not the beginning. But, come to think of it, 1,425 miles often represents the end of a trip for most riders.

I had noticed a rider in the parking lot in Salt Lake City who was wearing a helmet liner. The liner, which resembled a shower cap made of silk, was intended to prevent itching. I tried to buy one at Jim Plunkett's but none was available. I resolved to purchase a helmet liner as soon as I could.

At 5:00 p.m., Plunkett announced the standings and distributed rider packets for the next leg. At the end of the first leg, the standings (with a 4-way tie for 5th place) were:

STANDINGS AT SPOKANE

Standing	Rider	Motorcycle	Points
1	Gary Eagan	'94 BMW K1100LT	2,936
2	Rick Shrader	'94 BMW R1100RS	2,874
3	Ron Ayres	'95 BMW K1100LT	2,870
4	Steve Losofsky	'86 BMW K100RS	2,639
5	Ken Hatton	'91 Kawasaki ZX-11	2,621
5	Morris Kruemcke	'89 Honda Gold Wing	2,621
5	Eddie Metz	'85 Honda Gold Wing	2,621
5	Frank Taylor	'93 Yamaha FJ1200	2,621
9	Marty Jones	'92 Kawasaki Voyager	2,446
10	Boyd Young	'91 BMW K100RS	2,436

Committed Competitor

The highest-placed rider who hadn't tackled the Nebraska bonus was Steve Losofsky. Like Rick Shrader, Steve looks the part of a happy-go-lucky maverick. With long dark hair, mustache, and beard, Steve embodies the image of a free-spirited rebel who does whatever he damn well pleases. Those who know him will attest that the description fits. Steve looks the part. Not so his motorcycle.

Considering his ownership interest in Reno BMW of Sparks, Nevada, Steve was not riding the type of motorcycle I expected. His multicolored motorcycle started out as some form of BMW K100 and almost qualified as a "ratter." Parts of the fairing had been crudely cut away and two bottle mounts of the type attached to the frame of bicycles had been bolted into the inside of the fairing. Gauges were bolted to part of the framework and the original seat had been replaced with a wide "Police Special" solo seat. Steve had been riding the motorcycle for the last five years.

Steve owns Reno BMW with a partner, Jan Cutler. Both are well-known, and their customers include top riders from across the country. They take turns entering the Iron Butt Rally; one rides while the other minds the store. This time it was Steve's turn to ride.

In addition to being accomplished riders, Jan and Steve have done as much as anyone to promote endurance riding. For five years, Reno BMW sponsored a popular 24-hour endurance rally, the Nevada 1100. They no longer sponsor the rally, but remain active in endurance riding events.

During the last Iron Butt, Jan Cutler's performance provided one of the most interesting "I screwed the pooch" stories. Leading at the checkpoint in Spokane, Jan was so excited about the number of bonuses he had collected that he called Mike Kneebone from a motel in Gillette, Wyoming, to report, "I really have these guys now. I'll see you tomorrow night in Chicago."

"Perhaps you will," Mike replied. "But the checkpoint opens in the morning and will be closed by tomorrow night." After a long pause on the other end of the line, Mike heard Jan simply say, "I've got to go." Jan missed the Chicago checkpoint because he thought he had until 9:00 p.m., not 9:00 a.m., to get there.

Second Segment Strategy

The second leg began at 5:00 p.m. Wednesday in Spokane, and required riders to reach San Diego by 10:00 a.m. Friday, 41 hours later. Martin Hildebrandt decided to give the bonus packets another try. He opened the package and tried to locate the first few bonus locations on his maps. After 15 minutes of searching, he determined that the first three bonuses listed were too far from any route he would take to San Diego.

Martin returned to his strategy of hitting all 48 states. He plotted a route that would touch Oregon and Nevada and which would get him to San Diego, a distance of 1,360 miles, in the morning. Not aware of what the American deserts would have in store, he didn't know what an unreasonable objective he had set for himself.

After a brief look at the prospects listed in the new rider packet, I went directly to a first-class motel and rewarded myself with a hot shower, a big meal, and a few beers from room service. I hadn't planned on drinking beer during the rally, but I couldn't resist the temptation to celebrate the successful conclusion of the first leg of the rally. I'd have appreciated the celebration even more if I knew then that this would be the most relaxation I would have in the next ten days. Things were going to get a lot more rugged.

As I waited for dinner, I looked at the options. For the second leg, riders could choose a route through San Francisco, requiring them to face Labor Day traffic in Los Angeles and San Diego, or take a more direct route through the intense heat of Death Valley. Only a few of us selected a third option, which included the biggest "doable" bonus at the Custer Battlefield National Monument in Montana.

For me, the choice meant returning to Montana to the Little Big Horn Battlefield, where Lt. Colonel Custer's 7th Cavalry was annihilated in 1876 by the Sioux, Cheyenne, and Plains Cree Indians. I would then collect a bonus for purchasing gas in Buffalo, Wyoming, before pushing on to San Diego via Salt Lake City. The idea of devouring miles again in Montana was appealing. I would be in Montana during daylight and should have no interference from the law. But I was irked about retracing so much of the route I'd so recently traveled.

As I was preparing for four hours of rest, Bob Higdon was posting his review of our just-completed first leg. In his *Day One – Salt Lake City to Spokane, But How?* installment on the Internet, Bob described two "sensible" routes to Spokane. One was all interstate and the other all state routes, with higher scoring bonus opportunities.

He also described a third possibility:

> *Then again, if you're a true hero of the Lawrence of Arabia mold, you might consider the 315 point bonus at Chimney Rock, Nebraska, but no one in his right mind would do such a thing. Ride 1,400+ miles in the first day of an 11-day butt-breaker? Spare me.*
>
> *No, spare Gary Eagan, Rick (Swamp Thing) Shrader, and Ron Ayres. They not only made the ridiculously out-of-the-way trip, but they made it to the Spokane checkpoint before the window closed. It is a story for the Iron Butt ages. It is also the story of three guys who, I predict, will have almost certainly depleted their reserves to the point that no recovery is possible. Ardys Kellerman and Morris*

Kruemcke rode to Los Angeles from Fort Worth on the first leg of the '93 Butt by way of Louisiana and, while they were heroes for a day, both were time-barred at the next checkpoint and subsequently disappeared so far down the drain that not even the Roto-Rooter man could find them.

Although written in jest, it was just as well I wasn't aware that such a respected figure in the motorcycling community had already written me off.

BMW K-bike riders performed well on the first leg. This group photo before the rally shows, kneeling: Charles Elberfeld (left) and Gary Eagan (right); standing, left to right: Ardys Kellerman, Horst Haak, Tom Loegering Jr., Eric Faires, Robert Ransbottom, Boyd Young, Eddie James, Mike Stockton, Ron Ayres, Karol Patzer, Steve Losofsky (behind Patzer), Kevin Mello. Lyle the Bear is in front of Patzer.

Leg 2 – Spokane to San Diego, Author's Route

4

Spokane to San Diego

1,360 miles – 41 hours

Shifting into Second

The only time during the rally that I had a headache was after awakening at midnight on Wednesday in Spokane. I took an aspirin and hoped this wasn't the beginning of aches and pains that would interfere with my performance. I blamed the head-

September 1995						
Mon	Tue	Wed	Thur	Fri	Sat	Sun
28	29	30	31	1	2	3
4	5	6	7	8	9	10
11	12	13	14	15	16	17
18	19	20	21	22	23	24
25	26	27	28	29	30	

ache on the beers and short sleep. This single aspirin was the only drug I used during the 11 days. I didn't drink another beer until after the rally.

Only my high beam was functional, so I replaced the bulb with the spare I had packed. I still had only a high beam. I suspected a faulty switch and planned to replace it as soon as possible. I lost an hour fussing with the bulb but was underway by 1:00 a.m.

As I crossed into Idaho from Washington, the right glove box cover flew off the motorcycle and landed on the roadway. Apparently I had failed to latch it properly the last time I opened it. I stopped, parked the bike on the shoulder of the road, and walked back to retrieve the lid. As I approached, an 18-wheeler appeared and smashed the lid into oblivion.

I discovered an unexpected benefit to losing the lid: with the cover off, I was able to store three or four bottles of drinking water in the compartment. I'd been using the camel back device I'd brought with me, but it was annoying to struggle to remove it for refills, as it was difficult to get the thing on and off over the Aerostich. Now I could flip the lid of my Duo-Tech helmet and drink directly from bottles.

I felt chilly while traversing Lookout Pass on the border between Idaho and Montana. I had already switched my electrically heated handlebar grips to the "full hot" position. By the time I reached Missoula I was shivering and stopped to add another shirt, an electrically heated vest, and long underwear. I still had to traverse the high altitudes and freezing temperatures of the Homestake and Bozeman Passes before descending to the warmer Montana prairie on my way to the Custer Battlefield National Monument.

Eagan's Early Error

When Steve Chalmers announced the 48-state bonus at the dinner in Salt Lake City, Gary Eagan decided to pursue it. After leaving Spokane, he headed east on I-90 and stopped at the Idaho and Montana border to take a picture of his motorcycle parked beside the "Welcome to Idaho" sign. Forty miles later he arrived at Cataldo, Idaho, reached behind the seat, and realized he hadn't replaced the towel in the side compartment of his auxiliary tank cover after taking the photograph at the border. He reversed direction and headed back toward Montana, doubting he would find the towel. He felt his chances of winning already slipping away.

When he arrived at the location where he had taken the photograph, the towel wasn't to be seen. He walked down the highway about 20 yards and discovered the towel blown up against the concrete divider separating the traffic lanes. Gary retrieved his towel and headed south for Death Valley.

One would think he would be unlikely to forget the towel again. One would be wrong.

Gary was following a route which Bob Higdon would later suggest, in his Internet story for the day, as the only way to run the leg. In the account, *August 31, Day Two – The Valley of the Shadow of Death,* Bob wrote:

> *I think there's only one way to run this leg; I'm just glad I don't have to do it.*
>
> *It requires steaming right down the middle of the desert from Spokane for the bonuses in Reno and Tonopah, averaging 55 mph all night and all the next day. If you can average more than 55, you might be able to grab an hour's sleep. If you average less, you're sunk.*
>
> *It is critical that you reach the Death Valley visitor center before it closes at 1700 on Thursday. For this bonus you need an actual park stamp from that building; a picture of the park's sign, normally acceptable evidence, here is insufficient. Now, at last, you can sleep for ten hours (if you can find a motel room), arise at 0300 on Friday, and slog the last 350 miles to arrive in San Diego by 1000.*
>
> *Steve Chalmers has been thinking about these problems for two years. It took me three hours with a 486/33 desktop computer, Automap Pro, and a 16-ounce Dr. Pepper to work through it. The riders, dazed from the first day's ride to Spokane, will have somewhat less time to make their decisions.*
>
> *Somewhat.*

Eddie Errs Early, Too

I was following Eddie Metz back to Montana for the Custer Battlefield bonus, but Eddie was more than eight hours ahead of me. He arrived at the monument at 3:00 a.m., took the photo of his towel on the visitor sign, and headed for San Diego via Salt Lake City. Half an hour later, as Eddie went through his mental checklist, he realized he had left the towel hanging on the monument sign. He returned to the historic site to retrieve it, and headed for South Valley Yamaha in Sandy, Utah.

Meanwhile, Charles Elberfeld was 1,000 miles to the west, collecting some goodies at the Cycle Logical BMW dealer in

Eugene, Oregon, another bonus stop. Those who selected this bonus received Gatorade, sausage sticks, energy bars, and crackers.

When I reached the Custer Battlefield site just before noon, I pulled up to the ranger at the visitor gate and asked if other riders had visited before me. I heard a refrain I would hear often during the next ten days: "Yeah, there was a guy here on a motorcycle about an hour or so ago. He entered the park to get his passport stamped."

The bonus called for either taking a picture of the nearby park sign or having a National Parks Passport stamped. The stamp required a visit inside the park. After consulting the bonus listing to be sure it didn't require the stamp, I placed the motorcycle by the visitor sign, draped my towel across the motorcycle, captured the shot, and left.

I headed south on I-90 to Buffalo, Wyoming, collecting a bonus for purchasing gas at the same station where I had nearly run out 30 hours before. I continued to Casper, took a short cut over the 6,250-ft. Muddy Gap to Rawlins, and picked up I-80 west to Salt Lake City. I was approaching Rock Springs, Wyoming, as the sun was setting in front of me. An amateur photographer with several quality cameras, I regretted not being able to pack one. I would have liked to capture the dramatic sunset I was riding into.

Plenty of Places to Park

Just after midnight, some 130 miles south of Salt Lake City, I became sleepy and checked into the Iron Butt Motel at Fillmore. This time the Iron Butt Motel was the parking lot of a convenience store.

The Iron Butt Motel is the term endurance riders use for sleeping on one's motorcycle. Some riders do it by leaning forward, using their tank bags as a pillow. I was most comfortable leaning back. Anyone who has difficulty believing that it's possible to sleep on a motorcycle just hasn't been that tired.

The Iron Butt Motel has a lot to recommend it. It's easy to find, the rates are great, there's always a vacancy, and there's no problem about having to park your motorcycle out of your sight while you sleep. And you don't have to awaken a clerk if you want to check in at 4:00 a.m.

There are a few disadvantages, too. You never seem to be able to find one when it's raining, and there generally isn't a shower nearby *unless* it's raining. They are some of the dirtiest places going. There's no service to speak of. Security isn't great.

After placing the motorcycle on its centerstand, I arranged my duffel bag behind me to support my back. This is the classic position depicted on T-shirts designed several years ago by veteran rider Gary Moore, who is credited with coining the term "Iron Butt Motel." The shirts still show up occasionally at Iron Butt gatherings.

Although I usually sleep remarkably well this way, this time I had trouble falling asleep, not because of discomfort, but because of the constant banging of a chain against a nearby flagpole. After I inserted plugs into my ears, I quickly fell asleep. I no longer heard the racket of the chain against the flagpole. I also didn't hear my watch alarm.

While I was sleeping on my motorcycle, Tom Loegering was fast asleep in the comfort of his own bed in Manhattan Beach, California. For Tom, the trip to the second checkpoint in San Diego would be an easy two-hour drive down I-5 in the morning. He hadn't collected many bonus points yet, but he was refreshed.

The second leg may not have turned out so well for Tom if he hadn't made the bonus stop at Reno BMW during the day. He discussed his intention of going to San Francisco to pick up the bonus at the Golden Gate Bridge. Jan Cutler advised him that this was a "sucker bonus" and that he could be time-barred in San Diego if he tried it. The rule specified that the rider get a toll receipt dated after 2:00 a.m. The rider would then have to drive through rush hour traffic in Los Angeles to get to San Diego by the time the checkpoint opened at 10:00 a.m. Tom heeded the advice and passed on the Golden Gate bonus.

Sweltering Slowdown

By midnight, Martin Hildebrandt had already arrived in San Diego and was checking into a motel for the evening. Due to some minor misfortunes, he arrived more than 12 hours later than he had planned when he left Spokane.

First, Martin had discovered that the road he chose was under construction. He would have to take a detour. The detour placed him in the unenviable position of traveling for miles in deep gravel. After waiting at a railroad crossing in the middle of nowhere for a stopped freight train to clear the tracks, he decided to turn around and try to find another way to I-84. Instead of saving time, he became hopelessly lost.

Near Echo, Oregon, Martin finally ascended the access ramp onto I-84. The combined effects of riding so many miles in soft gravel and being lost had fatigued him. He stopped at a motel in Twin Falls, Idaho. After three hours of sleep, he continued south. Once the sun came up, it got hotter and hotter until he felt that he was running against a giant flame thrower. At every fuel stop he drank half a gallon of water, but still could hardly replace what he was losing to perspiration.

Shortly after leaving Ely, Nevada, the thermometer on his motorcycle was indicating 118°F. This was the hottest weather he had ever experienced. Pan-Galactica gave up, not able to withstand the heat any longer. When he attempted to drink from the container that he was carrying in his black duffel bag, he nearly burned himself. The sun had already gone down when he reached Barstow, California, but the thermometer was still indicating over 115°F.

He finally arrived in San Diego half an hour past midnight. He had been totally battered and drained of energy by the ride through the intense heat but was at least able to get a good night's sleep before checking in at Brattin Motors in the morning.

Tempted to be Tardy

I slept for about two hours at that first Iron Butt Motel—an hour longer than I'd intended. When I awoke at 2:00 a.m., Rick Morrison, an international flight attendant with American Airlines, was returning to his motorcycle with a cup of coffee in his hand. Rick was running late after having an accident in a construction area near Sheridan, Wyoming. He was thrown from his motorcycle when his front wheel sank into deep gravel. Although the fairing was damaged, the motorcycle was still operative. Rick lost a few hours trying to arrange for the state to accept responsibility for the accident, on the basis that the hazard was improperly marked.

September 1995						
Mon	Tue	Wed	Thur	Fri	Sat	Sun
28	29	30	31	1	2	3
4	5	6	7	8	9	10
11	12	13	14	15	16	17
18	19	20	21	22	23	24
25	26	27	28	29	30	

Rick, who was also returning from the Custer Battlefield route, thought I was sleeping too late to make the checkpoint in San Diego. Rather than disturb my sleep, he thoughtfully went into the convenience store to ask the clerk how long I had been asleep. "I know that guy's going where I'm going, and I'm worried about getting there in time," Rick remarked to the attendant. The clerk searched for my gas receipt to determine when I had arrived at the station.

I awoke just as Rick approached to wake me up. I thanked him for his thoughtfulness, put my helmet and gloves on again, and did a quick review of the requirements for the ride to San Diego. I had a little more than 600 miles to go and about eight hours to get there. I left the parking lot knowing I would have to burn some fast tanks to San Diego. I left Rick behind to finish his coffee. I would have felt rude for not offering to ride with him, but Gregg Smith got me off the hook during the orientation meeting.

"Riding together isn't recommended or expected. You'll both get tired, but at different times, so you'll have to stop more often. And it gives you too much to worry about. You can't help but get distracted trying to keep tabs on your companion," reasoned Gregg.

These have always been my sentiments anyway. I enjoy riding solo much more than riding in a group, even a group of two, unless the disadvantages are second to other pleasures, like riding with one of my sons.

Despite Gregg's advice, there were a few twosomes who attempted the ride together. These included the father and son Loegerings and the husband and wife Langs. A few others teamed up and rode together after meeting on the road. Hank Rowland and Horst Haak wound up riding the remainder of the rally together after meeting at a gas station during the first leg. Suzy Johnson and Chuck Pickett rode most of the way together after meeting at the bonus location in Klamath Falls. But the most notable twosome was Ron and Karen McAteer—riding two-up on the same motorcycle.

Disturbed at having overslept in Fillmore, I realized I could have used one of Ed Otto's "Screaming Meanie" timers. He describes it as "my best friend . . . a device guaranteed to get you thrown out of any motel in the world. It also does an excellent job of waking you up." A truck driver whom Ed met at a diner introduced him to the Screaming Meanie before the rally. This small device permits you to enter the number of minutes you wish to sleep before an alarm sounds. When the timer sounds, it can wake the dead.

Picking a Place to Pause

I was checking out of my Iron Butt Motel in Fillmore while Charles Elberfeld was checking into his, 500 miles to the south. Charles had undergone what he later described as his most intense experience of the rally as he was making his way from the Los Angeles area to the checkpoint in San Diego.

Around midnight Charles was north of Los Angeles, dead tired and wanting an opportunity to stop to rest. But his concern about being able to make it through the traffic in Los Angeles to reach San Diego on time caused him to try to get through Los Angeles before stopping. Thinking that he had missed a turnoff to stay on I-5, he tried to cheat the highway by crossing the white demarcation lines, hit an unknown obstacle, and went airborne.

The short flight and abrupt landing awakened him enough to realize that he was heading in the wrong direction on I-5. When he exited the freeway to examine the damage to the motorcycle, he entered an area that he described as a "war zone," replete with refugees, burned out hulks of automobiles, and abandoned buildings. He quickly returned to the interstate.

When he stopped at a gasoline station a little farther on, the attendant was sitting in a bulletproof cage. As he dismounted he heard the voices of several youths running in his direction from a half a block away. Leaving the refueling for later, he jumped back on the motorcycle and once again returned to the interstate.

It was nearly 3:00 a.m. when he stopped at a roadside rest area about 35 miles north of San Diego. Although he was planning to rest on the ground near his parked motorcycle, he spotted a dozen large rats gathered around a trash receptacle. Too tired to continue without sleep, and satisfied that no one had a gun pointed directly at him, he checked into the Iron Butt Motel. An hour of sleep refreshed him enough to continue to San Diego.

While Charles was having these difficulties, Ed Otto was about to be ticketed by an Idaho State Trooper for running about 50 mph slower than most riders were traveling. He would have chalked up another Iron Butt first for doing 37 mph—8 mph below the legal minimum. This was the most "Floppy" was able to manage while climbing the hills on the way south. The officer decided to let Ed off with a verbal warning.

Ed headed his Helix back to Salt Lake City for the easy bonuses and the direct Death Valley route, along with Bob Honemann on his vintage BMW. This leg was the end of the rally for Bob when his crankshaft bearing came apart near Butte, Montana.

Brian Bush, head of the film documentation crew, who was planning on doing only the first two checkpoints, overslept in San Francisco. Brian, the only rider to opt for the western route through San Francisco, would probably have been time-barred in San Diego even if he hadn't overslept. The traffic on his way to San Diego would almost certainly have delayed him.

Ron Major was having a relatively easy ride so far. He selected a fairly direct route to San Diego, stopping for a bonus gas receipt in Los Angeles, a photograph of a monument at San Juan Capistrano, and a parking receipt from the San Diego International Airport. He reported fog so thick at San Juan

Capistrano that he had to take four photographs before he had one that satisfied him.

San Diego Stopover

The 150 miles from Fillmore to Hurricane, Utah, provided me an opportunity to regain time lost during my nap. Relatively refreshed and riding a great road in the dead of night, I was able to make great time.

Approaching Hurricane, Utah, I wondered if the name of the city had been chosen because of high prevailing winds. The wind was buffeting the motorcycle as I entered the area and continued through the winding interstate coming into the Virgin Valley area. When a heavy cross-wind unexpectedly slammed into the motorcycle, I was temporarily startled, but the bike seemed to respond automatically by leaning steeply into the wind. These gusts nearly moved me a lane's distance several times.

The wind died before I crossed Moab tribal lands north of Las Vegas. By then, I was wishing for their return to cool me down.

I arrived at Brattin's BMW in San Diego just after 10:00 a.m., only three minutes into the window, after driving through San Bernardino with some of the fastest commuter traffic I've ever experienced. At less than 80 mph, I would have been overrun.

The mechanic at Brattin's changed my oil and verified that my dimmer switch wasn't working. He didn't have a replacement, so I called Barb and asked her to alert George Mitmanski, the BMW mechanic in Plano, that I needed a new switch. The next leg would take me through the area, and I had extracted a commitment from George to open the shop on Sunday to change my tires. Now he could do some warranty work too.

Brattin's was a great host. They provided several submarine-style sandwiches, each six feet or so in length. I found a helmet liner and bought a new pair of leather gloves as well. I was happy to provide some business to the checkpoint operator.

A lot of motorcyclists and interested non-riders came to Brattin's to see the motorcycles, talk to the riders, and take pictures. The riders felt like celebrities. Ed Otto's Helix and Martin Hildebrandt's GPS-equipped motorcycle drew the most attention.

I was astonished at the standings in San Diego. I was in second place and began to feel that I could finish in the top ten. I set a goal for being in the top three and identified Gary Eagan as a rider who would probably remain there.

Based on appearance and performance, Gary seemed a threat. His motorcycle was rigged for a major conquest, with auxiliary fuel tank, large water tank, long-range driving lights, and radar scrambler. With the help of a Salt Lake City manufacturer of camping equipment and knapsacks, Gary had designed a custom covering for his auxiliary fuel tank that included an integrated one-gallon thermos to store drinking water, pockets for keeping soft drink bottles at hand, and additional storage pockets. Next to Ed Otto's Helix and Martin Hildebrandt's ST1100, Gary's motorcycle drew the most attention.

Morris Kruemcke probably would have upstaged even Ed and Martin if he had brought his "project bike" to the rally, rather than his Gold Wing. He surprised riders when he arrived in Salt Lake City without the black "Stealth Bike" that had been such an attraction at the Iron Butt Pizza Party in Daytona, Florida, the previous March. Morris's Stealth Bike started as a wrecked Gold Wing but no longer had much in common with the production version. The bullet-shaped vehicle, enveloped in a jet-black carbon-fiber skin, looked as if it belonged either on the salt flats of Bonneville or in a James Bond flick. Mounted inside, the cockpit surrounded the rider and included such space-age instrumentation as a digital fuel flow readout as well as the more pedestrian tachometer and speedometer. Some sort of backrest had been modified to support the rider's chest as he leaned forward to stay below the wind stream. This reduced rider fatigue and increased mileage at the same time. And yes, this bike was also equipped with the "Morris Kruemcke Pee-Tube."

This bike also had an array of PIAA high-intensity driving lights that virtually turned night into day. "It's the damnedest thing," Morris drawled, in his thick Texas accent, a large cigar suspended between his lips. "When I flick these babies on, all life in front of the motorcycle is frozen in its tracks. Deer, elk, moose, rabbits, you name it. Nothing moves. But as the critters fall out of my 'light cone' as I pass them, they get unfroze, go nuts and jump in some entirely unpredictable direction. It scared the hell out of me the first time I passed a big buck like that and could see it jumping directly at me as I passed it. It isn't a problem so long as you're moving along. By the time the animal drops out of the beam and makes the jump, you're at least 100 feet or so on down the road."

When I asked Morris why he hadn't brought the Stealth Bike, he talked about the unpredictability of the Iron Butt Rally: "Well, that bike works great so long as I'm making my way down the road at a decent clip. But if Chalmers decides to send me up Pikes Peak or gets me stuck in traffic in some god-forsaken oven, the cooling system won't work well enough to keep the motorcycle running properly. It's still a project bike and I still have some things I have to do to it before I run it in the Butt."

I also found in San Diego that Frank Taylor, Eddie Metz, and Ken Hatton had selected the same eastern arc to the Custer Battlefield that I had traveled. Rick Morrison made it too, but was late in arriving. Just north of Los Angeles he was stopped for speeding. Rick was so tired that it took ten minutes for him to notice the trooper following him with lights flashing. Fortunately for Rick, he was only exceeding the limit by about ten miles per hour.

"I don't mean to be a nag," said Steve Chalmers as Rick approached the check-in desk, "but you need to be more careful about getting to these checkpoints on time."

"Hey, I'm married and I know what nagging is," Rick shot back, in good nature. "You *are so* nagging."

I noticed a pattern to the behavior of the riders at the checkpoints. After dismounting and turning in their paperwork, they next tried to determine who was yet to arrive. I looked for Leonard Aron's '46 Indian Chief and wondered if the bike would make it through the entire rally. He made the checkpoint, but with only 18 minutes to spare. Considering the condition of the bike's clutch, many riders doubted that the Indian could survive the next 2,700-mile transcontinental leg to Ft. Lauderdale.

Martin Hildebrandt arrived early and decided to repair his broken computer equipment. With the computer disassembled, Martin's motorcycle was inoperable. Ron Major offered Martin the use of his motorcycle to ride to a nearby Radio Shack to buy parts.

Tom Loegering moved up from 19th to 15th place on his leisurely ride from Spokane. After a good night's sleep in his own bed near Los Angeles, Tom appeared capable of closing the gap during the transcontinental leg. Tom's son had had enough and dropped out.

Counting Calamities

Rick "Swamp Thing" Shrader made it to San Diego late. He had been in second place in Spokane, but he dropped to fifth in San Diego.

Skip Ciccarelli, who had been time-barred in Spokane after striking a deer, had been unable to secure the parts needed to repair his motorcycle. He would not make the San Diego checkpoint and would therefore be relegated to "DNF" (Did Not Finish) status. Riders missing more than one checkpoint could not qualify as finishers. Steve Attwood, too, struck a deer after he left Spokane and dropped out of the rally.

A stone thrown by an oncoming truck on a desolate stretch of U.S. Highway 50 west of Delta, Utah, eliminated Steve Losofsky. First reports were that the stone broke Steve's leg after it passed through the lower fairing of his motorcycle. We learned afterward that the leg was just badly bruised.

STANDINGS IN SAN DIEGO

Standing	Rider	Motorcycle	Points
1	Gary Eagan	'94 BMW K1100LT	5,951
2	Ron Ayres	'95 BMW K1100LT	5,866
3	Frank Taylor	'93 Yamaha FJ1200	5,751
4	Eddie Metz	'85 Honda Gold Wing	5,688
5	Rick Shrader	'94 BMW R1100RS	5,573
6	Ken Hatton	'91 Kawasaki ZX-11	5,484
7	Morris Kruemcke	'89 Honda Gold Wing	5,439
8	Eddie James	'93 BMW K1100RS	5,398
9	Marty Jones	'92 Kawasaki Voyager	5,329
10	Rick Morrison	'95 BMW R100RT	5,191

Two Gold Wing riders held positions in the top ten during the first two legs: Eddie Metz and Morris Kruemcke. Here is the 'Wing contingent before the rally, left to right: Jerry Clemmons, Morris Kruemcke, Kevin Donovan, Brad Hogue, Jim Culp, Harold Brooks, Doug Stover, Eddie Metz, and Chuck Pickett.

Bob Higdon's *Day Three – The Inside Line* dispatch included the following remarks:

Five riders—Ron Ayres, Frank Taylor, Eddie Metz, Ken Hatton, and Rick Morrison—each took the alluring eastern arc to the Custer Battlefield in Montana, averaged 3,000 bonus points, and added 2,000 miles to their bike's odometers over the course of 41 hours. It is reported that in San Diego they looked like Chernobyl refugees.

Contrast their experience with that of Gary Eagan, the leader of the pack at Spokane, who took the inside route straight to Death Valley as your scribe suggested. He too rang up 3,015 points on the second leg, though riding 350 fewer miles and catching seven hours sleep near San Diego before the checkpoint opened. With an entire continent to cross in the next 75 hours, should we bet on Eagan or AyresTaylorMetzHattonMorrison? What to do? What to do? I only wish roulette were this easy.

Rallymaster Steve Chalmers had arrived to work the checkpoint. At noon he distributed rally packets and encouraged riders to collect the nearby "gimme," the Coronado Bridge.

Spectators watched as riders spread maps on the sidewalk to plan their routes. I planned mine working on the back seat of the motorcycle, while one spectator engaged me in conversation. He asked why we ride like this if there isn't prize money, and what happened to entry money if big prizes aren't awarded. I tried to be polite, but I was brief. I didn't have time to become involved in a lengthy discussion, and he wouldn't have understood anyway.

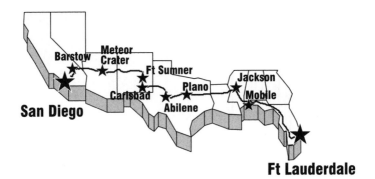

Leg 3 – San Diego to Ft Lauderdale, Author's Route

5

San Diego to Ft. Lauderdale

2,660 miles – 75 hours

The Longest Leg

The most direct route from San Diego to Ft. Lauderdale is east on I-10. I decided to go north first, to I-40, collecting bonuses in Laughlin, Nevada, and Needles, California. These more attractive possibilities included Meteor Crater, Fort Sumner, Carlsbad, and Waco, Texas. I'd also be able to stop in my home town, Plano, Texas, for service on my motorcycle.

I headed for the Coronado bridge with virtually every other rider for an effortless bonus. Because motorcycles normally use the bridge for free, the first riders reaching the toll plaza had to insist on paying the toll to get a receipt.

After pocketing my receipt, I headed north on I-15 for the Mojave, our nation's largest desert, and Barstow, California, where I could pick up I-40 for the trip east. It was just after noon on Friday morning and I would have to do almost 2,700 miles by 6:00 p.m. on Monday, Labor Day.

The desert was hot. By the time I reached Barstow at 3:00 p.m., it was windy and small drops of rain were streaming across my faceshield. I was exhausted and wanted to time my passage through the rest of the desert for the early morning to avoid the higher temperatures that typically crush inexperienced riders. I checked into a motel.

I ordered a pizza and called Barb to discuss my plans and ask her to fax me some outputs from Automap Pro, a software package for route planning. I had already selected my intended route, but I wanted Barb to verify that my time and distance calculations were reasonable.

Several years earlier when Mike Kneebone was our house guest, he suggested that a rider could benefit from having a "pit crew" at home. The support team could help develop and refine strategy by assessing the rider's decisions while the rider rested. But I liked the Iron Butt's individual nature. I liked an event in which participants perform their best without help. I questioned whether such help was sportsmanlike and within the rules.

Mike assured me that this type of assistance was fair. "After all, the real challenge is to ride the miles legitimately, and a pit crew can't do that for you from the other end of the phone. If you ride the miles and don't secure an advantage that's unavailable to other riders, you'll be fine. Besides, a lot of riders will have laptop computers so they can examine options on the fly."

As I grabbed a few hour's sleep at the motel in Barstow, Barb began assessing my options. Before leaving the motel, I stopped by the office to collect the Automap Pro printout she had faxed. The outputs from Automap Pro confirmed that what I had planned was reasonable.

Casino Chips to Craters

I left Barstow at midnight on Friday and headed for Laughlin, Nevada, to pick up a casino chip from the Colorado Belle Casino. According to my atlas, the most direct route to Laughlin was a small secondary road that ran north from Needles, California.

September 1995						
Mon	Tue	Wed	Thur	Fri	Sat	Sun
28	29	30	31	1	2	3
4	5	6	7	8	9	10
11	12	13	14	15	16	17
18	19	20	21	22	23	24
25	26	27	28	29	30	

I could collect the casino chip and use the same road to return to Needles, collect a gas receipt, and continue east on I-40.

I discovered that one of the delights of the rally is the occasional unexpected discovery of a previously unknown but interesting location. Laughlin, a small Nevada gambling town four miles south of the Lake Mead National Recreation Area in the southeastern tip of Nevada, was such a location. Although it was dark, I was impressed with the cleanliness of the town, named after Don Laughlin, former owner of the 101 Club in Las Vegas. He bought a boarded-up motel and 6.5 acres of land in 1964 and opened a casino. A U.S. Postal Services Inspector insisted that Don give it a name in order to receive mail. Don recommended the names Riverside and Casino, but the postal official used Laughlin instead.

When I reached the casino, I asked the doorman to watch over my unattended motorcycle. I rushed inside, passing black-jack tables, roulette wheels, and rows of blinking, jangling slot machines on my way to the cashier's window. I purchased a gambling chip but had difficulty hearing the cashier over the noise of so many levers being pulled and released and coins being discharged from the machines. After finally discerning, "Your friends were here earlier," I smiled, pocketed the prized chip, and dashed for the door.

I retraced my route to Needles through this hot, dry region in the Mojave Desert, the geographic meeting point of Nevada, Arizona, and California. Jagged peaks and ravines created by volcanic activity eons ago give the territory a forbidding, alien landscape. The Colorado River slices a sharp crevasse through the desert as it rushes toward the Gulf of California carrying the snow runoff from the Rocky Mountains. I arrived in Needles at 3:00 a.m. for the bonus gas stop, then continued east toward Flagstaff and the Meteor Crater bonus.

As I made my next fuel stop in Kingman at 5:00 a.m., Fritz and Phyllis Lang were pulling into a rest area in Arizona. They had stopped the day before during the heat of the day and were on the road again at 11:00 p.m. By 5:00 a.m., Fritz was tired, but Phyllis was wide awake. As she waited for Fritz to awaken, she enjoyed watching the sun rise from behind the Saguaro cactuses beside the highway.

Fritz had more reason than normal to be tired. He had been released from the hospital just a week before the rally after experiencing heart problems. Prudence would have dictated a longer period for convalescence, but Fritz was determined to participate in the rally. He wouldn't have the opportunity again for at least two years.

Pursuing Penetrating Points

The Meteor Crater National Landmark, located less than 40 miles east of Flagstaff, is billed as the earth's most "penetrating" natural attraction. Some 50,000 years ago, a huge iron-nickel meteorite struck the rocky plain with an explosive force greater than 20 million tons of TNT. The meteorite, an estimated 150 feet across, left a crater more than 500 feet deep, more than 4,000 feet wide, and 2.4 miles in circumference, large enough to accommodate 20 football fields.

A Museum of Astrogeology there features a number of meteors and meteorite fragments and displays films and exhibits depicting the wide-ranging effects of the meteor's devastating impact. A NASA Apollo space capsule is also available for inspection in Astronaut's Hall of Fame. To collect the Meteor Crater bonus, a rider could either take a photo of the Apollo space capsule or save the entrance receipt to the national landmark.

Ron Major was waiting in the parking lot as the gates opened at 6:00 a.m. He had collected the bonus at the south rim of the Grand Canyon and had stopped at a motel in Flagstaff to sleep for a few hours. As he left Meteor Crater, he saw Rick Shrader entering the area, riding on a flat front tire. Rick had also visited the Grand Canyon but had hit a curb while distracted by his search for a visitor sign to the park. It damaged both his wheels. After collecting the Meteor Crater bonus, Rick was planning to head for Tucson to buy new wheels.

I reached Flagstaff at 8:30 a.m., then descended several thousand feet to the desert plains and continued east to Exit 233 for the access road to the crater. It was a magnificent morning and I enjoyed the distant view of the San Francisco Mountains surrounding Flagstaff. I passed over deep, narrow Canyon Diablo, one of the most troublesome obstacles to the first efforts to build roads west through this region.

Ardys Kellerman's motorcycle was in the parking lot when I arrived. Ardys was preparing to leave, but we talked briefly. She told me there had been an accident at the Grand Canyon, referring to Rick Shrader, but that no one was injured. Within 24 hours, Ardys would herself ride her motorcycle off the interstate near Grant, New Mexico, and be hospitalized with injuries that would eliminate her from the rally.

After the rally, Ardys's friend and fellow Texan Morris Kruemcke remarked, "Ardys started the rally this year intending just to ride from one checkpoint to another. By the time she reached the second checkpoint in San Diego, she was ready to try to win the thing."

Shortly after Ardys and I left Meteor Crater, Rick Morrison arrived to collect his first bonus since leaving San Diego. At the San Diego checkpoint, Rick was so tired that he distrusted his ability to translate the countless bonus possibilities into a sensible plan. He knew he needed to head east, so he rode nearly 350 miles to Phoenix without so much as peeking at his rally packet. He saved that until he could rest.

On reaching Phoenix, Rick checked into a real motel for the first time since the start of the rally, nearly 72 hours earlier. After a good night's sleep, he studied the bonus possibilities and headed directly for Meteor Crater. When he arrived, he decided to improvise on his otherwise straightforward photographic chore. Rick enlisted a security guard to help him produce a photograph that would be unique among the several hundred created during the rally. Just before the guard snapped the picture, Rick dropped his pants and "mooned" the camera. Rick's towel was clearly visible with the spacecraft, but he wasn't certain the photo would be acceptable in Ft. Lauderdale. He chuckled as he thanked the guard for his help and pocketed his admission receipt, back-up evidence of his Meteor Crater visit.

Desert Distress

The Arizona afternoon was intensely hot—123°F at the gasoline station in Yuma where Ed Otto stopped. The cashier assured him that it wasn't over 114°. For the first time in his life, Ed found himself putting on extra clothing to ward off the heat.

Martin Hildebrandt reported, "I felt like I had fallen into a giant hair dryer."

Jerry Clemmons had just heard a nearby radio station announce 117°F, but he believed it was even hotter. He watched Eric Faires and Tom Loegering blast by him in their Aerostich suits. Jerry was trying to stay in his leathers, following Steve Attwood's advice dispensed at the riders' briefing several days before.

Unlike Ed Otto, Jerry decided to ignore the advice. "I figured these guys wearing the snowmobile suits out here will die real soon. I pulled into a rest stop where the drinking water smelled like a sewer. I was only there for the water. You don't ever have to take a leak when it's 120°F." He removed his leather jacket.

Horst Haak and Hank Rowland were in the Yuma desert in Arizona when Hank had to stop to replace his fuel filter—with his thermometer indicating 120°F. By the time they reached Gila Bend, Horst noticed that his knees were weak and he got the chills when he entered a restaurant. He had been accustomed to waiting until an hour before his next planned fuel stop before he drank water, to avoid filling his bladder.

"I wanted to kill two flies with one swat," Horst remarked. "It backfired on me and I learned from it. I began drinking enough to ensure that I wouldn't get dehydrated again."

The severity of the desert heat was reflected in Bob Higdon's next dispatch, *Day Four – It Only Hurts When I Laugh:*

> *Leaving San Diego at noon guaranteed that the field would storm into the Mojave Desert at the height of the mid-afternoon heat. A casual glance at the weather charts of the southwest offered no hope: It was criminally hot. Even normally scalding towns were setting records. One rider, Robert Fairchild, bailed out of the rally in Gallup, NM. He had come through Yuma at a boiling 113°F. It then became*

worse. He told Steve Chalmers that he couldn't take it any longer.

You can't blame Fairchild for a poor route choice. There are only three rational ways east from California: I-10, I-40, and I-70. You can't reach any of them without riding through a firestorm this weekend. For myself, I enjoy the heat. I'll turn on the electric vest at 70°F and don't feel comfortable unless it's at least 90°F. But I do recall that the one and only time I absolutely could not continue was on a day that was not as hot as it was in Arizona this afternoon.

Eddie James may be the only person enjoying the hellish weather. He made a wrong turn while in Death Valley and ended up riding through that nightmare twice. It was 118°F.

There is expected to be no significant change in the weather over the next few days.

Suzy Johnson and Chuck Pickett had been riding together since shortly after Spokane, when they met at the bonus location in Klamath Falls, Oregon. Leaving San Diego, they decided to take I-8 east to Casa Grande, Arizona, where they would stay with a friend of Chuck's for the evening. Suzy wasn't feeling well in the 120°F temperatures and had stripped down to jeans and a wet shirt with only a light windbreaker on top.

The brutal desert heat also debilitated Charles Elberfeld. He felt he hadn't taken proper care of his mind and body during the first two legs, so he decided to take the most direct route to Ft. Lauderdale and disregard bonuses. He wanted to use the leg to recover and regain his strength.

My ride east through Arizona included the Painted Desert and the Petrified Forest. Keeping the Aerostich unzipped, but on, while drinking constantly must have helped me endure the scorching desert conditions. The Aerostich is without question the single most important piece of motorcycling equipment I own. It can be worn in all weather conditions and provides protection if the body comes in contact with the road. I think the suit made this portion of the trip more tolerable for me than it was for other riders.

During the day Steve Chalmers learned Steve Attwood's deer strike was more serious than had first been believed: in addition to damaging his motorcycle, Attwood had suffered a concussion, broken ribs, and a fractured collarbone. The damage would have been worse if he hadn't been traveling at low speed.

This day marked the end of the rally for Ken Hatton. Ken attempted the giant 687-point bonus at Mount Rushmore, South Dakota, but a sprocket disintegrated on his ZX-11 "crotch rocket," putting him out of the rally. This was similar to the sprocket problem he encountered with the bike during the '93 rally, resulting in his third consecutive Iron Butt DNF. Ken was the eighth rider to drop out of the rally, behind Attwood, Ciccarelli, Fairchild, Honemann, Kellerman, Loegering, Jr., and Losofsky.

Roy Eastwood had to do some fancy riding to avoid a fall when the rear door of a tomato truck swung open and dumped a few hundred tomatoes in his path. It was one of many close calls reported by riders during the rally.

Enduring Ennui

After Arizona, the transcontinental leg was sheer drudgery for me. Martin Hildebrandt thought the route through Oklahoma and Kansas was boring as well. "It looks a lot like Nebraska to me, just worse," he reported. "It's wheat, wheat, some small house, then a silo with a fuel station and a small church at every second silo. This must be hell. Maybe that's why people seem so religious here."

For my own amusement, I had planned to listen to music, improve my Portuguese, and make a career decision. I had even packed cassette tapes for the trip, including hours of radio programs recorded in Portuguese, before I left Brazil. I had almost never used the bike's stereo system because I considered the quality pathetic at any reasonable speed. I equipped my helmet with speakers that let me pipe music from the bike's stereo system directly to my ears, a system I expected to enjoy while riding. Shortly after leaving Plano for Salt Lake City, though, I had decided the music was annoying. The radio and cassette player remained off for the duration of the trip.

It was questionable whether I would be needing Portuguese skills much longer anyway. My work in Latin America was coming to an end and the company had presented me with two totally different career opportunities. One required moving to Europe to assume responsibility for business development in Poland, Hungary, and the Czech Republic. The other was a Plano-based position with one of the company's largest business units. I planned to use this "vacation" to consider the alternatives.

I preferred Eastern Europe and was looking forward to the move, especially when I learned I could live in Switzerland. Now I wanted to figure out how to make Barb feel more enthusiastic about it. I expected to develop a persuasion strategy during the rally, but my thoughts almost never turned to work. With no music, no Portuguese, and no desire to think about work, I filled the long hours with daydreaming.

It's difficult to know how you are doing relative to other riders, as contact with them is so infrequent. Each rider rides his own rally and plots his own course, independent of competitors. Unlike most sporting events, riders get few opportunities to confirm their standing. Much is left to the imagination.

"How fascinating it would be to track the routes being ridden by 55 riders, with numerous combinations of bonus locations to chose from," I thought. I imagined we had been issued tracking devices that kept Steve Chalmers and Mike Kneebone informed of our locations in an Iron Butt Central Operations Center. Colored lines traced our routes as we traveled them across brightly lit plasma display screens mounted between our handlebars, as Martin Hildebrandt had installed Pan-Galactica. In the Central Operations Center, Steve and Mike watched our progress as the lines slowly meandered across a giant map of the United States projected onto the wall.

If such technology had been employed, a pattern would already have developed as the group departed Salt Lake City for Spokane, then progressed to San Diego. Upon leaving the checkpoint cities, the departing riders headed in three or four general directions. A few riders took the most direct route to the next checkpoint, with little or no apparent interest in bonus stops. As time for the window to close drew near, all riders converged on the next checkpoint, as if a giant vacuum cleaner had been switched on, sucking the riders to their common destination.

Although this was nothing more than an interesting fantasy that helped me amuse myself during the long hours on the highway, I thought about how soon we might see the introduction of the concept in the Iron Butt Rally. After all, with Martin Hildebrandt's "Star Wars" tracking equipment, we had already been given a glimpse of the future.

As I was passing through Albuquerque on I-40, Morris Kruemcke's motorcycle was parked at a rest area and Morris was lying down on the concrete nearby. Even though he thought he had been drinking plenty of liquids, he believed he was suffering heat prostration. He couldn't continue until he gave his body time to recuperate. Morris had come to Albuquerque via Torrey, Utah, and the Dixie National Forest. The Torrey stop was worth 341 points, but required traveling nearly 200 miles of scenic but torturous secondary roads. Eddie Metz also had opted for the Torrey bonus and reported that the road was so twisty that he used all the rubber on the sides of his tires and none from the middle. "The ride from Cedar City, Utah, to Torrey is probably the most crooked road I have ever been on," Eddie marveled.

After refueling in Torrey, Eddie headed for Kansas and Morris headed for New Mexico. Somewhere between Kansas and Florida, Eddie began to doubt that he could make it to Ft. Lauderdale in time for the one-hour window. He stopped to call his wife to report that he was going to say "the hell with it" and head home. "Carrie told me to get my ass to Ft. Lauderdale on time, because she wasn't going to live with me for the rest of her life having me say 'I wish I hadn't dropped out of the rally.' It's a good thing I called her because I made it to Ft. Lauderdale with an hour and a half to spare."

Instead of heading south for Albuquerque, Morris would have done much better on this leg if he had stuck with Eddie. Morris didn't realize this mistake until after the rally.

Picking up the Pace

When I reached Santa Rosa, I headed south for Fort Sumner to photograph the grave of Billy the Kid. Route 84 from Santa Rosa to Fort Sumner was great—two lanes, straight as an arrow, through the desolate prairie with visibility to the horizon. It was possible to drive fast relatively safely. I could see for miles and there was nowhere for troopers to hide. This was an ideal place to open it up. A highway worth revisiting. My kind of place.

Sometimes, while driving at high speeds, I think about people who ask how fast riders drive on endurance rallies. I'm reluctant to discuss the speeds we reach because it's so difficult for people to understand how we can regard it as safe. It just isn't possible, to many people, ever to justify driving at triple-digit speeds, much less on a motorcycle.

For what it's worth, I rationalize something like this. First, neither I nor most riders I know drive through populated areas faster than most motorists, perhaps 10 miles per hour over the limit. I reserve my speeding for wide open spaces, in good weather, with good visibility and no other traffic on the road. I don't drive fast when my tires are low on tread, and I keep my motorcycle in top condition. If anything goes wrong, I'm likely to be the only person injured. Carelessness is a self-correcting problem.

The thought kept occurring to me, as desolate as the route to Fort Sumner was, that there *couldn't* be much here in the middle of nowhere. There wasn't. Fort Sumner has nothing to boast about except the grave of Billy the Kid. The town seems to have a lot invested in the cost of maintaining a museum, but it's hard to imagine there's enough traffic to justify the cost. It was desolate. I photographed the grave behind the museum and acquired another 72 points.

Gary Eagan preceded me through the area by several hours. After capturing his photo of the grave site, he once again forgot to pack his towel before leaving. At least this time he discovered the oversight and returned for the towel after riding only 15 miles or so.

When Gary arrived in Hereford, Texas, a few hours later, he stopped at a gas station in the midday heat to apply drops to his dry, burning eyes. He was standing by the motorcycle trying to apply the drops, but they didn't seem to be helping. Then he realized that he hadn't removed his sunglasses.

"Drops were streaming off my glasses and onto my leathers," he recalled. "I looked up and saw a woman standing there, holding the hand of her son. They were staring at me as though I was from Mars, decked out in full leathers in searing heat while pouring drops on my glasses and laughing like a jackass. They were still standing there, staring, when I rode off laughing."

From Fort Sumner, I headed south through Roswell, Artesia, and Carlsbad to reach the Carlsbad Caverns National Park. Darkness fell as I arrived in Carlsbad. As I rode through the slow local traffic, creeping from one signal to another, I tried to remind myself to be especially alert, particularly near intersections. I usually avoid being on the motorcycle on Saturday nights because of the high percentage of drivers who are under the influence of alcohol. The real danger wouldn't begin for a few more hours, though, and I planned to be back on the safer interstate highways by then.

Carlsbad Caverns National Park, the "Eighth Wonder of the World," contains 83 separate caves, including the nation's deepest limestone cave. The caverns are located within a Permian-Age fossil reef among the rugged Guadalupe Mountains. The wide and gentle Pecos River flows through the town of Carlsbad, enhancing the beauty of the area.

I found the visitor sign at the entrance to the park and snapped a photograph for another 72 points, then headed for Hobbs, New Mexico, entered Texas, and turned south at Lamesa to intersect I-20 at Big Spring.

Holiday Hush

After midnight on Saturday, the interstate was as desolate as I can ever remember seeing it. When I reached Colorado City, I worried about being able to find

September 1995						
Mon	Tue	Wed	Thur	Fri	Sat	Sun
28	29	30	31	1	2	3
4	5	6	7	8	9	10
11	12	13	14	15	16	17
18	19	20	21	22	23	24
25	26	27	28	29	30	

gas. It was Labor Day weekend and most travelers had completed their trips. Because of this, many stations that would normally have been open were closed. I finally found a station with an automated credit card reader at the pumps and was able to buy gas, even though the station was closed.

Departing San Diego for Ft. Lauderdale, most riders passed through the great state of Texas at more or less the same time, though a few took a slightly more northerly route through Kansas and Oklahoma, and two were as far north as South Dakota.

About 125 miles to my southeast, and several miles east of Fort Stockton, the Langs pulled into a rest area for a nap. They passed through Fort Stockton believing that they would find a motel a little farther down the road. Seeing none, they opted once more for a rest area and found Suzy Johnson and Chuck Pickett asleep on picnic tables as they arrived.

Bob Higdon's daily Internet posting, *Day Five – Go East, Young Man,* commented not only on the riders, but on the role of the rallymaster:

> *One of the incidental victims of the rally is the rallymaster himself, Steve Chalmers. He'd probably be better off without a telephone, but he is perverse enough to have one and when it rings, he answers. It's rarely happy news.*
>
> *Leonard Aron on the 1946 Indian called Chalmers from Houston. The bike is holding up better than he is. He has discovered that the ordinary routines of daily road life have become a cryptic puzzle. It is Agonie de Butt, a common pathology. You stand at a gas pump eating a bacon cheeseburger with extra cholesterol. Suddenly you cannot recall if the burger should go in your mouth or get stuffed in the tank. Though he will be time-barred in Florida, Leonard's mood remains obstinately gleeful. He will try for Maine.*

Ed Otto, like Hank Rowland and Jesse Pereboom a short time before him, was stopping on the Helix to visit the Alamo. He met Jim Culp in front of the old mission and the two riders took turns holding each other's towel while the other snapped

Leonard Aron and his 1946 Indian Chief. Indian motorcycles haven't
been manufactured since 1953.

Rallymaster Steve Chalmers working the checkpoint in San Diego.
Most of Steve's work during the rally took place in his Salt Lake City
"command center."

the needed photograph. When Mike Kneebone learned that Ed was still stopping for bonuses, he was incredulous. Mike insisted Ed was crazy for going after any bonuses at all.

After taking his photograph of the Alamo, Jim prepared to leave—without his rider towel. Ed ran to him as he was departing to return the towel he had dropped on the road. Jim, a member of MENSA, demonstrated that a genius-level IQ is no protection from fatigue-related carelessness.

Marty Jones was also in Texas, nearly 600 miles south of me, spread across the hood of a police cruiser—in handcuffs. A law enforcement officer himself, Marty had been stopped for speeding. When the officer asked to see his driver's license, Marty explained that his license was in a fanny pack that was stuffed near the front of the windshield of the motorcycle, along with his gun. After the officer cuffed Marty and located the gun, he finally responded to Marty's assertion that he too was a law enforcement officer.

The officer, apparently regretful after treating a fellow lawman so shabbily, tried to engage him in conversation. Marty just wanted out of the cuffs. When released, he headed for Louisiana.

Gains Gone (with the Wind)

After stopping in Abilene at 5:30 a.m., I forgot to close the zippers to my tank bag. Somewhere between Abilene and Fort Worth, the bank deposit bag containing my receipts, casino chip, and photos of bonus locations blew away. I had a severe sinking feeling as I searched through all of my belongings, realizing I had lost all evidence of my ride. The irony was that several times during the rally, I had thought about how tragic such an incident would be.

I've had a lot of time to reflect on this tragedy since the rally. Leaving the bag unzipped was not simply carelessness. My body and mind were pushed beyond the limits of endurance by heat, stress, and lack of sleep. Some riders refuse to pay the price and drop out. Others pay in injury. I paid the wind.

I bought gas again at Fort Worth, earning myself a paltry 18 bonus points. After losing hundreds of points for the hundreds of miles between there and San Diego, these 18 points seemed of little value. I called Barb to report the tragedy. She suggested that we leave the motorcycle in Plano for the scheduled tire change and oil service, and go back to look for the receipts. This seemed a good idea at the time.

I met Barb at the BMW dealership, where George Mitman-ski had agreed to open the service facility on Sunday. We made the trip back to Abilene in our car, looking for the bag of receipts along the highway, but the 8-hour search was in vain. In retrospect (and now knowing the receipts wouldn't be found), I should have used the time to sleep and to go after the 162-point bonus at the Dr. Pepper Museum in Waco, Texas, as I had originally planned.

I managed to sleep a little while Barb drove. Though less comfortable than my bed, it beat the Iron Butt Motel. Even though I planned to have the motorcycle serviced in Plano, I never intended to crawl into my own bed for sleep during the service interval. I live only ten minutes away from the shop, but I planned either to find a place to lie down inside the shop or to sleep in a car in the parking lot. I had heard the Persinger story. Paul Persinger and his son had been the first father and son team in a previous Iron Butt rally. During the rally, they decided to stop and sleep in their own beds. They overslept and missed many of the bonus points they had been targeting. They had been doing well, running near the top of the pack, until this mistake.

Something mysterious seems to occur when a rider, after completing a week of 1,000-mile days, is reintroduced to his own bed. It breaks his momentum, dissolves his focus, and ruins his concentration. Although Tom Loegering had spent the second night of this rally in his own bed in California, he hadn't yet subjected himself to the merciless sleep deprivation that makes exchanging a comfortable bed for more punishment so difficult.

When Barb and I returned to Plano, George had serviced the motorcycle, closed the shop, and returned home, leaving the motorcycle in the parking lot. While Barb picked up a McDon-ald's lunch for us, I went to South Fork Ranch for a 27-point bonus. I was familiar with this bonus location from the TV program *Dallas,* as it's a short distance from my home. My company has often sponsored dinners and other social events at the ranch.

While I was collecting the South Fork bonus, Barb tried to purchase a flashbar for the camera but was unable to find one. Rather than purchase a Polaroid camera for the rally, I had borrowed an old model. I struggled through with the borrowed camera, but later learned that the type of flashbar the camera required to take photographs at night was almost impossible to find.

Freshened up for Florida
After Barb and I ate in the car, I headed for Ft. Lauderdale with fresh oil, new tires, a high and low beam headlight, and a 500-point deficit. For the next week, I would be plagued by a recurring "if only" feeling that would be felt by most of the riders before the ordeal was over.

"If only I could turn back time and do that segment over again. If only I had zipped my tank bag."

I wasn't the only rider who had a problem holding on to receipts. Fritz Lang had lost his and his wife's receipts in California the day before, but found them after backtracking while Phyllis waited beside the road. I didn't learn until a year after the rally that Chuck Pickett also lost receipts on this leg. According to Suzy, who was riding with him at the time, Chuck lost them after stopping in Pumpkin Center, Louisiana.

As I was stopping for gas and another 15 bonus points in Shreveport, Louisiana, Jerry Clemmons was hours ahead of me but was missing an easy 18 points at the USS Alabama. After visiting the 434-point bonus location in far-away Brownsville, Texas, Jerry was concerned about his ability to make the Florida checkpoint in time. Although he was aware that he was passing the USS Alabama bonus in Mobile, nothing would have made him leave the interstate at that point except an empty gas tank. Also, he knew the bonus was a very small one.

Ed Otto was already at the battleship site with Ron Major. Other riders who stopped included Karol Patzer and Eddie James. Karol had passed Eddie a short while before, noticing his motorcycle parked on a side road while he performed vigorous calisthenics. Eddie flew past Karol and met up with her again at the battleship.

Restless Respite

I made Delhi, Louisiana, at a little past midnight on Sunday and stopped in Jackson, Mississippi, for an 81-point gas stop at 1:30 Monday morning. I left the interstate at Jackson and headed southeast on U.S. Highway 49, toward Hattiesburg.

September 1995						
Mon	Tue	Wed	Thur	Fri	Sat	Sun
28	29	30	31	1	2	3
4 ★	5	6	7	8	9	10
11	12	13	14	15	16	17
18	19	20	21	22	23	24
25	26	27	28	29	30	

Shortly after leaving Jackson I became tired. Rest areas were uncommon along this route but I continued, hoping to find one. Finally, when I didn't feel able to continue, I turned onto a leaf-covered dirt road leading away from the highway and into the woods. I decided I would be safe if I backed the motorcycle off the road far enough to be hidden from traffic. I placed the motorcycle on the centerstand and assumed the classic "Iron Butt Motel" position once again.

I had an uneasy feeling as I tried to sleep. Even brightly lit rest stops aren't safe in the "wee hours" of the morning. I wondered if I shouldn't have followed Barb's advice and brought a weapon with me. I know that several riders always include a firearm on rallies. This was one time I wished I had done the same.

I couldn't have slept for more than half an hour when I realized I was so uncomfortable in this location that I was wasting time to stay. I continued toward Florida, not stopping to sleep again until the checkpoint in Ft. Lauderdale. I intended to pick up U.S. Highway 98 at Hattiesburg to Mobile, Alabama, but missed the turn and rode to Gulfport instead, adding 50 miles to the length of my trip to Florida.

A Case of Coincidence

Michael Stockton had a more pleasant experience on U.S. 49 twelve hours earlier. He was stopped by a Mississippi State

Trooper. Usually, being stopped for speeding isn't pleasant, but when Michael handed over his driver's license, he noticed that the trooper wore a college ring from the University of Mississippi. A good friend of Michael's, now a doctor in Oklahoma City, had attended the same university. When Michael mentioned this, the trooper acknowledged with surprise that she and Michael's friend had been best friends in high school and college.

"Did you have a big, black Harley Dresser in the mid '80s?" she asked.

"Yes," Michael replied.

"Well, your friend told me about you. She suggested that you and I meet some time, because I ride motorcycles too."

After talking for half an hour, Michael explained the Iron Butt.

"Well, let me help you make up some time," she suggested. "I'll escort you out of the State of Mississippi."

So Michael received a high-speed escort to the Alabama state line.

When Michael told me this story, it reminded me that the most incredible coincidences I have experienced have occurred while I was on a motorcycle. A year before my chance meeting with Mike Kneebone in 1991, Barb and I were touring the Colorado Rockies. We rode the motorcycle to the top of Pikes Peak, near Colorado Springs. As we were walking back to the Harley from the coffee shop, I heard the distinctive Baltimore accent of a woman standing by a group of other motorcycles. As I turned to look at her, I recognized my cousin Betty. She and her husband, whom I had never met, were touring on a Gold Wing. Neither of us knew that the other had developed an interest in motorcycles in the ten years since we had last seen each other. We exchanged warm hugs, introduced our spouses to one another, and took a few photographs to document for our families that we had met. It provided both of us with an extraordinary vacation story to relate upon our return home.

Like Jerry Clemmons before me, I didn't take the three-mile side trip at Mobile to collect the 18 easy bonus points at the USS Alabama. I was already concerned about making the Ft. Lauderdale checkpoint on time.

I pushed on to Pensacola for a measly 21 bonus points, arriving shortly before 9:00 a.m. As I entered Florida just after sunrise, I could tell there had been rain in the area before I arrived. I knew that most riders were ahead of me and wondered if the previous night's rain had delayed them.

Gary Eagan's experience the previous evening may have been a unique one. As he pulled into a gasoline station near Hoxie, Arkansas, lightning was flashing in all directions. He was surrounded by clouds, could smell the rain in the air, and felt the wind blowing in strong, sustained gusts.

Half an hour later, trucks started blinking their lights as they went by in the opposite direction. Gary believed the trucks were trying to warn him of a trooper, but he wasn't exceeding the speed limit at the time.

"A massive gust of wind pushed me off the road, across the shoulder, and into a field," Gary reported. "I didn't know what hit me. The field was muddy, but not yet so bad that I couldn't get back on the road. As I looked to the northeast, I could see a small funnel cloud. It scared the hell out of me."

Awaking Alarmed

Martin Hildebrandt also experienced difficulty with the severe weather. His GPS computer equipment had conked out on him again before he even reached Los Angeles. So he continued without it through Arizona and New Mexico and into the Texas panhandle at Dalhart. He crossed into Colorado to add the state to his 48-state quest, then crossed Oklahoma and proceeded to Kansas, Missouri, and then south to Florida.

When Martin crossed into Florida he ran into heavy rain. By 3:00 a.m. he was exhausted from riding through the rain in the dark for so long. He found himself making no more than 30 mph and knew it was time to sleep (a standard warning sign of severe sleep deprivation for endurance riders is when they find themselves unable to maintain a steady, safe speed).

He hadn't seen a motel in some time and didn't know how long it might be before he found the next available one. He had packed a hammock, but he didn't know where he might be able to hang it to stay dry and safe. Like most German tourists, he had been warned about stopping at rest areas in Florida and wasn't aware that all of these areas were now patrolled by security guards. So Martin decided to make his first visit to the Iron Butt Motel.

He pulled the motorcycle under an overpass, as far out of the way as he could manage, laid his head on the tank bag, and spread his arms across the fairing. Despite the pounding rainstorm, he fell asleep immediately. About three hours later, startled awake by a truck roaring past, he thought he had momentarily fallen asleep while riding and was about to smash into the concrete bridge abutment a short distance before him. He tried to execute an emergency swerve, nearly toppling himself and the motorcycle to the pavement.

"The emergency braking got my adrenaline flowing and I headed off relatively refreshed," Martin related.

I was still 600 miles and nearly ten hours from the Ft. Lauderdale checkpoint by the time I made Cottondale, Florida, at 10:30 a.m. Martin had already visited with Mike Kneebone in Ft. Lauderdale and had checked into the motel across the street from the Burger King checkpoint for five hours of sleep before the checkpoint opened.

I stopped for gas in Madison and crossed the Suwannee River a short time later. I've crossed that river a dozen times during the last 30 years or so, and each time, the state song of Florida, Stephen Foster's "Old Folks at Home," begins running through my head. When I begin singing the song to myself, I usually continue doing so for hours. This time, I sang it until I reached the Everglades Parkway four hours later.

By 2:30 p.m., when I was entering Wildwood, Jerry Clemmons was also in Ft. Lauderdale, suffering a panic attack for misplacing *one* of the gas receipts he collected on his way from San Diego. I wish I had been there to tell Jerry about missing receipts. After Mike Kneebone advised him to calm down and return to his motorcycle to look for the missing receipt, Jerry found it blown against some shrubbery where he had unloaded his motorcycle.

Then Mike turned to Rick Morrison and began validating his bonus evidence. He wasn't prepared for Rick's shot of the Apollo spacecraft at Meteor Crater. Clearly visible were Rick's rider towel, the Apollo spacecraft—and Rick's bare white buttocks.

"I don't think we can accept this Apollo 'moon' shot," Mike said as he chuckled at the photograph. "But it's OK, I see you've included your entrance receipt too."

Murf's wife Rena was arriving at the Ft. Lauderdale checkpoint on a "clean underwear supply run" for her husband. She happened to be visiting her aunt in West Palm Beach, less than 50 miles away. When murf arrived at the checkpoint, he was so certain he would finish that he asked his wife to ship his tuxedo to Salt Lake City when she returned to their home in St. Louis. Anticipating trouble obtaining Dom Perignon champagne on short notice in Salt Lake City, murf shipped an order of it from Ft. Lauderdale.

Flirting with Forfeiture

It would be difficult for me to make Ft. Lauderdale on time. I was driving fast and had selected the west coast Florida route to bag 86 points for crossing the Everglades Parkway. The highway, which crosses the largest remaining sub-tropical wilderness in the contiguous United States, is whimsically referred to as "Alligator Alley." Many people know that the 1.5 million acre Everglades is home to alligators, but are surprised to learn that the animal life also includes cougars, panthers and crocodiles. The Everglades is the only area in the United States where alligators and crocodiles exist side-by-side.

Approaching the toll booths at the eastern end of the parkway, I was in trouble on two counts: I was running out of gas and I was running out of time. The Ft. Lauderdale checkpoint was only open for one hour, and it had begun shortly after I got *on* the Everglades Parkway. I was losing five points each minute and risked missing the checkpoint altogether. Worse, I didn't know how to get to the checkpoint from the parkway.

The instructions described how to get to the checkpoint, a Burger King, by riding south on I-95. It didn't specify how to get there if approaching from the west. I gave the I-95 exit number to the toll collector and asked for directions. He sent me the wrong way at a time when I could least afford a delay. I realized the mistake when exit numbers headed in the wrong direction. I tried to turn back, certain I would deplete my remaining fuel before I reached the checkpoint. The same cursed feeling that I had recently experienced upon discovering the loss of my receipts overwhelmed me.

Rick Morrison, a member of American Airlines's international flight team, provided an interesting "moon shot" of an Apollo space capsule to capture 168 bonus points at Meteor Crater, Arizona.

"If only I had driven two or three miles per hour faster, I wouldn't be having this problem. If only I could relive the last several hours. If only I hadn't been asleep at the switch back in Hattiesburg and missed the turnoff for Mobile." And especially, "If only I had synchronized my watch with Steve Chalmers's at the start of the rally."

I was showing 6:55 p.m., less than five minutes from being time-barred. I didn't know if my clock was faster or slower than Steve's, but I was certain I would blow the checkpoint if I stopped for fuel. I finally reached the proper exit and had to stop again for an eternal red light at the foot of the ramp. The Burger King was now within sight, but my watch indicated I was already late. I could almost feel Florida's state bird—the mockingbird—sitting on my shoulder and living up to its name as I sat baking in the "Sunshine State."

Three-time Iron Butt finisher Gary Moore was responsible for clocking riders as they pulled into the checkpoint. When he saw me approaching the parking lot, he approached me with a smile on his face, displaying the stopwatch. There was less than one minute remaining before the window slammed shut. When the crowd realized I was a contestant, an encouraging cheer rose from across the parking lot. Thanks, I needed that!

A few minutes later, riders gathered around Kneebone, who was preparing to distribute rally packets. My fuel pump was making so much noise from being starved that I wondered if there was something wrong with the motorcycle.

I had written off the Florida checkpoint and thought the best I could do would be to qualify as a finisher, assuming I did OK on the rest of the rally. What a pleasant surprise to find that all I had to worry about was the tremendous loss of points and the severe penalty for being so late in Ft. Lauderdale.

When I left San Diego more than 40 hours earlier, I was in second place behind Gary Eagan. My lost receipts and penalty for tardiness at the Ft. Lauderdale checkpoint permitted five of the "Big Dogs" to squeeze in front of me. Now, a full week since the start of the rally, I was in seventh place behind Eagan, Metz, Jones, James, Kruemcke, and Young. At least I was in the top ten.

STANDINGS IN FT. LAUDERDALE

Standing	Rider	Motorcycle	Points
1	Gary Eagan	'94 BMW K1100LT	9,263
2	Eddie Metz	'85 Honda Gold Wing	9,117
3	Marty Jones	'92 Kawasaki Voyager	9,108
4	Eddie James	'93 BMW K1100RS	8,920
5	Morris Kruemcke	'89 Honda Gold Wing	8,789
6	Boyd Young	'91 BMW K100RS	8,557
7	Ron Ayres	'95 BMW K1100LT	8,487
8	Rick Morrison	'95 BMW R100RT	8,458
9	Eugene McKinney	'94 BMR R1100RS	8,426
10	Ron Major	'94 Honda ST1100	8,413

Rick Shrader, Frank Taylor, Fritz and Phyllis Lang, and Leonard Aron were time-barred in Ft. Lauderdale. Frank made it to Mount Rushmore, South Dakota, nearly 1,400 miles from San Diego. Finding himself nearly 2,200 miles from Ft. Lauderdale, he gave up his triple-digit pace when he realized that even that wouldn't enable him to make it without being time-barred. Gary Gottfredson got sick on this leg and was also out. Leonard, after putting 5,300 miles on his Indian Chief during the last five and a half days, had burned a hole in a piston in Georgia. The others reported that they would attempt to pick up with the group in Maine.

Although Rick "Swamp Thing" Shrader wasn't injured in his accident at the Grand Canyon, the mishap started a chain of events that led to his third DNF. After the rally, Rick recounted his accident:

"I went to the south entrance of the Grand Canyon and couldn't find a single sign that said 'Entrance,' so I entered the park and was standing on the pegs looking back over my shoulder when a curb crawled out in front of me. It launched the motorcycle and bent both wheels. I rode 200 miles with a flat front tire and the rear hopping around all over the place. I stopped at Meteor Crater, then tried to make Tucson where I could buy new wheels, but I didn't make it. I spit the front tire off and had to wait at a service station while friends brought me $2,000 worth of replacement parts.

"By the time I was able to get going again I was 12 hours behind schedule, hot and exhausted. When I reached eastern New Mexico, I heard truckers talking on the CB about two Iron Butt riders that were killed. I stopped and called Steve Chalmers to find out what was going on and was told I was hearing things.

"I figured there was no way I could make up the time, but Steve told me to get my ass to Florida. I tried. I don't even know what state I was in when I pulled off the road, lay down, and slept a couple of hours. When I finally did get to Florida, I only had six hours to make 600 miles. I decided to drop out and head back to Utah. I spent a day resting up in Florida and took the time to visit a cousin before heading back."

To Rush or to Rest

After the rally packets were distributed at 7:00 p.m., many of the riders hurried on their way in pursuit of the new challenges. Martin Hildebrandt was conferring with a local group of CISsies about hitting each of the states along the eastern seaboard as he made his way north to Maine. For some reason, Martin came to the United States convinced that there was a state named Providence and was trying to reconcile it against the map. A visiting CISsie finally persuaded him that there wasn't any such state.

For me, it was time to check into a motel once again. I took a quick look at the challenges between me and Maine and headed for the same motel where Mike Kneebone and the checkpoint workers were staying. I visited Mike's room to deliver my receipts for the previous leg, meager as they were.

Mike suggested doing the "big bonus" at Ft. Kent, Maine, and getting to Gorham in time for eight hours of sleep before starting the final leg back to Salt Lake City. As tired as I was, it didn't take long for me to decide I couldn't do it.

"What is Kneebone trying to do?" I thought. "Does he want to sabotage my ride for some nefarious reason?" Apparently, Mike thought he could have accomplished it had he been competing. Or perhaps it would have surprised him to learn that I hadn't been to bed since Barstow, California—more than 70 hours earlier. Other riders must have come to the same conclusion, because the Ft. Kent bonus went unclaimed. Mike insists it would have been a winner.

During my conversation with Mike, I told him a bolt had vibrated loose on the luggage assembly. He taught me an important lesson: duct tape can fix almost anything on a motorcycle until proper repairs can be performed. In the early Iron Butt rallies, when time-consuming tire changes resulted in hefty penalties, several riders wrapped duct tape around threadbare tires for the last several hundred (or thousand) miles.

Years before, when Mike Kneebone and Fran Crane were accomplishing their record-breaking 48-state tour, they were delayed when an airplane ran out of fuel and landed on the highway. The police had closed the road and Mike had placed his motorcycle on its sidestand near the airplane. When refueling was complete and the engine of the aircraft started, the prop wash blew the motorcycle over, breaking the windshield and cracking the fairing on Mike's motorcycle. He fixed things with a roll of duct tape and the journey continued. I made a note to include duct tape on my checklist for future rallies.

I made plans to cross the Chesapeake Bay Bridge Tunnel and continue through New England via Dover, Delaware, collecting as many bonus points as I could along the way. If I had known that Bob Higdon had again suggested that I might wind up an also-ran, I might have been less enthusiastic about continuing. His dispatch for the day, *Day Six – Time on Their Hands,* stated:

> *It could be worse. You could show up at 19:01 and lose about eighteen hundred octobillion points, condemning you to the "also-ran" category and ensuring that e-mail will let people around the world know how you screwed the pooch.*

> *Ask Ron Ayres, the hard-charger who was in second place in San Diego. Not only did he come within 120 seconds of being shut out in Florida after a 4,000-mile ride, he managed to lose all his receipts between San Diego and Abilene, Texas, because he didn't zip his tank bag. So much for those bonus claims. The way his ride is turning, he's probably fortunate that he wasn't arrested for littering.*

I walked a short way to a McDonald's for a Big Mac dinner before returning to the motel.

While preparing to grab a few hours of sleep, Suzy Johnson looked on as members of the Christian Motorcycle Association repaired her motorcycle. She had encountered some rough roads in Louisiana and broken part of the exhaust system. The Christian volunteers were on hand at the checkpoint to help with the repairs. Suzy hadn't been in bed since Arizona and wanted to sleep, but the Christian bikers wanted to talk. So Suzy talked until midnight, when the repairs were complete. Then she checked into a motel and collapsed for the evening.

Seeking Shelter

The riders who left immediately after the rally packets for the fourth leg were distributed had the worst problem with the side effects of Hurricane Luis, which was pelting northern Florida with wind and rain. The storm pounded the Caribbean island of St. Martin so badly that its residents named a potent cocktail after it. Some riders were grounded by the heavy rain in St. Augustine. Charles Elberfeld and three other riders sat under a bridge for an hour and a half, along with a handful of cars.

Eddie Metz pulled to the side of I-95 to don his rain gear after receiving a warning over his CB radio from a southbound trucker: "Hey, northbound Gold Wing, you're gonna be gettin' real wet in about 20 minutes." The advice was appreciated, but Eddie's stop to don the rain gear caused a minor catastrophe.

"All of a sudden, I found myself lying in the grassy shoulder of I-95 with the bike on its side. 'What the hell happened?' I thought. I lost one of my gloves and my helmet had rolled into a ditch. I got on the CB to call for help in picking up the motorcycle, which fell over when I apparently neglected to put the sidestand all the way down. A highway patrolman and a motorist stopped to help."

After continuing to St. Augustine, Eddie found at least two inches of water on the road. He pulled into a Chevron station for a few hours to wait until the rain subsided.

Harold Brooks, a veteran endurance rider with 40,000 Iron Butt miles under his belt, was deluged south of St. Augustine and had to peer over his windshield to see the edge of the road. Since he was going only 40 mph, he decided to sleep through the rain and make up lost time afterwards. He stopped at the next motel he could find.

Harold had learned to be more cautious about letting himself get too far into the hole after he wrecked his motorcycle in Mina, Nevada, and banged himself up as he was approaching the end of the 1991 Iron Butt. "It's something that haunts me often," Harold told me. "It completely destroyed the bike and even today, more than four years later, my shoulder still aches. I was in fifth place, less than 150 miles from the finish, when it happened. If not for this, I would have a perfect finish record. I redeemed myself somewhat in 1993, when I was able to pull off a fifth place finish. Hell, that was like a victory to me."

There was a roof over the entrance to the motel office; the clerk invited Harold to leave his motorcycle under it, where the clerk could keep his eye on it while Harold slept. Harold's room was on the other side of the building, so he grabbed everything that he needed and pocketed the room key. He patted the key in his pocket several times on the way to his room to be sure it was still there, but when he finally reached his room, he reached into the pocket and extracted . . . a candy bar.

"I searched but never could find the key," Harold reported. "I had to go back to the office and ask for another one. The only thing I can figure is that I must have been so tired and distracted that I ate the key, thinking it was a bar of candy."

On leg three, 1991 Iron Butt winner Ron Major made it into the top ten. In addition to Ron, several other riders piloted Hondas; they are, left to right: Ron and Karen McAteer, Garve Nelson, Michael ("murf") Murphy, Martin Hildebrandt, and Ron Major.

Leg 4 – Ft Lauderdale to Gorham,
Author's Route

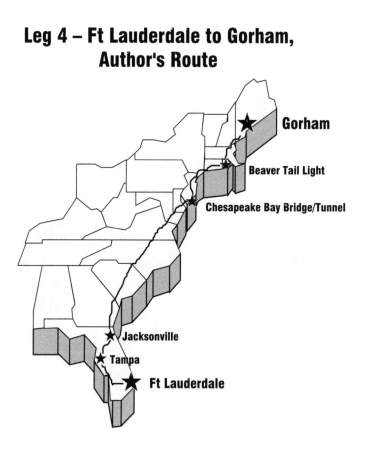

6

Ft. Lauderdale to Gorham

1,590 miles – 46 hours

Seven Days Down

In Ft. Lauderdale, I rose at 2:00 a.m. after six refreshing hours of sleep to begin the eighth day of the rally. My next rendezvous was to be in Gorham, Maine, at 6:00 p.m. on Wednesday, 40 hours away. I packed the motorcycle, bought gas, and crossed

September 1995						
Mon	Tue	Wed	Thur	Fri	Sat	Sun
28	29	30	31	1	2	3
4	5	6	7	8	9	10
11	12	13	14	15	16	17
18	19	20	21	22	23	24
25	26	27	28	29	30	

Alligator Alley for the second time in eight hours, this time for a 141-point bonus. At one of my next fuel stops, I bought duct tape and another flashlight, then tried somewhat successfully to repair the luggage rack with duct tape and bungee cords.

Credit Crunch

As I was trying to get out of Florida, the Langs were still trying to make it to the Ft. Lauderdale checkpoint in heavy wind and rain. They had called Steve Chalmers the day before to report that they would not be able to make the checkpoint on time. But to preserve their opportunity to qualify as finishers, they would have to show evidence that they visited Ft. Lauderdale, and they had to be on time in Gorham and Salt Lake City.

In addition to the miserable weather conditions they were enduring, they were suffering a misfortune that occasionally befalls unsuspecting travelers: Their credit card stopped working. They couldn't use it to pay for gasoline, food, or lodging, nor could they withdraw cash from ATM machines, even though Phyllis had deposited sufficient money in their account to cover their trip.

Many travelers are unaware that credit card companies will shut off access to their accounts if their spending patterns deviate significantly from their usual habits. The Langs' card, showing multiple small purchases in succession across the country, had triggered a security program alerting their credit card company to suspicious-looking activity.

Most banks try to contact the customer before disqualifying the credit card. My bank called Barb to report suspicious activity on our card. They asked if our card had been lost or stolen, noting that purchases were being made in many states in a 24-hour period. Barb informed the bank that I was touring the country and that the purchases were valid.

The Langs' bank made no such call, and when Phyllis tried to call the bank, she got only a recording saying the bank was closed for the holiday weekend. So they continued toward Ft. Lauderdale, unable to buy food for fear that their limited cash would be gone and they would be unable to purchase fuel needed to reach the checkpoint. It wasn't until they reached Ft. Lauderdale that they could persuade a clerk at a gasoline station to advance them $50 so they could last until they could correct things with their bank.

While the Langs were trying so desperately to reach Ft. Lauderdale, Suzy Johnson and Chuck Pickett were preparing to leave. Suzy and Chuck started the day in high winds accompanied by heavy rain. It wasn't long before they realized the best they would be able to do on this leg would be to arrive in Gorham two hours after the checkpoint closed. Suzy considered giving up, but wanted to be the first woman to finish the Iron Butt on a Harley-Davidson. They forced themselves to continue.

Semi- Squeeze

Meanwhile, Martin Hildebrandt was approaching Washington, D.C., contemplating which states he should visit on his trek to Maine. While in Oklahoma two days before, he decided to complement his high-tech approach to the rally with a low-tech touch. He had purchased a yellow highlighter and began coloring states already visited on his AAA map. Referring to the map, he decided that he should make an excursion into West Virginia to complete that entry in his "coloring book." He soon became entangled in one of the incredible traffic jams common to the Washington area.

"I was in the middle of a giant traffic jam leading through Washington to the horizon," Martin reported. "I decided to do what had worked well for me in other places in the rally and began splitting lanes. This worked for several miles until I found myself between a semi and a truck that was pulling a mobile home. I could see the semi driver's face in his rear view mirrors, so I knew that he had seen me.

"The driver began to pull over, smashing me into the mobile home. I was attempting to maintain my speed to keep the motorcycle upright as I was being held against the side of the moving mobile home. When the semi finally began to fall back, the lug nuts of the truck's front axle sheared the right cover off my motorcycle's engine guard.

"When I managed to finally clear the semi, I jumped the motorcycle onto the sidewalk and stopped to examine the damage and to give my knees an opportunity to stop shaking. In addition to the damage caused to the motorcycle, my left leg, which had been pinned against the side of the mobile home, was wracked with pain. I decided that weeping wouldn't help anything. The semi was gone, so I continued on my way to West Virginia. This was the last time that I practiced lane-splitting in the United States."

Capitol City Concerns

Martin finally captured photographic proof of his West Virginia visit and headed east again for Washington. Not realizing that the District of Columbia was not a required "state," he began looking for a gasoline station in Washington.

"Finally, I spotted a fuel station from the interstate, took the exit, and turned into the parking area. I felt that I had entered some 'end of time' scenario. The station wasn't very old, but was damaged with signs dangling and people hanging out. All pumps except one were occupied. I parked at this pump and found that two of the three handles were unusable. One had a hand-printed sign, 'out of orda,' hanging on it, and the other had been cut. Apparently, someone had tried to set it on fire.

"I tried to use the remaining handle, but found that I had to enter the station to pay for the purchase before the pump would function. On entering the station and having an opportunity to inspect my surroundings, I began to understand why prepayment was required.

"The cashier was surrounded by bulletproof glass and there were several signs stating that the station would not accept bills over $20. One sign stated, 'In No Case Is There More Than $50 Cash Here.' As I stepped from the cashier's window, I detected at least 20 pairs of eyes locked on me. Although all pumps were occupied, I didn't see any vehicle taking fuel while I was there. All vehicles were at least ten years old, and all had some major body damage. After quickly taking a gallon of fuel, I departed. I was careful to not make eye contact with anyone. I had the impression that the small package that I saw being exchanged with the driver of one of the parked cars was not containing vitamin pills."

Martin saved his coloring book assignment for later and hurried back to the highway to continue his trip to Maine.

Drenched, not Drowned

By the time I left the Tampa/St. Petersburg area on the way to Jacksonville, raindrops began to spatter across my windshield and the faceshield of my helmet. I moved the electrically-operated windshield all the way down to let the full force of the wind blow the rain from my faceshield, to improve visibility.

It was raining heavily when I reached Jacksonville at 10:30 a.m. Many of us were still riding through the tail of the hurricane and rain was coming down in sheets at a 45-degree angle. On I-95, in the midst of a convoy of 18-wheelers, my motorcycle suddenly and unexpectedly stopped running! I glanced quickly at the emergency "kill switch" to check if I had accidentally bumped it, but I hadn't. I had been passing traffic in the far left lane and had to make a dicey exit across three lanes of traffic to the right shoulder of the highway. This was the scariest thing I've ever had to do on a motorcycle. Ever!

I was certain this was the end of the rally for me. I anticipated having the motorcycle trucked to a shop for repair. Thank God for the cellular phone. It was about 10:00 a.m. in Plano, so I called my mechanic, George Mitmanski, to see if he could help. As the phone rang, I held my breath. The way my luck was running, he wouldn't be there.

George answered. When I explained the situation to him, he responded, "Ron, before doing anything else, put the side stand up and down a few times." I asked him to stay on the phone while I tried this. The motorcycle started immediately.

"The safety switch that's supposed to prevent the engine from being started while the side stand is down sometimes shorts out in rain," George explained.

Thank you, George. Thank you, God. Thank you, thank you, thank you!

I resolved to disconnect this unwelcome "safety feature" and do something nice to thank George at the end of the rally. How ironic that the single most dangerous thing that happened to me during the rally was the fault of a safety feature. This is a great example of a feature introduced by manufacturers, probably at the insistence of some government bureaucrats, that has the potential to cause more serious problems than it purports to prevent.

Aside from the malfunctioning headlight **dimmer** switch I had replaced in Plano two days earlier, this was the LT's first hiccup, and I didn't really blame it on the bike.

Robert M. Pirsig, in his classic bestseller *Zen and the Art of Motorcycle Maintenance,* insisted that each machine has its own unique personality which could be defined as the intuitive sum total of all you know and feel about it. "The new ones start out as good-looking strangers and, depending on how they are treated, degenerate rapidly into bad-acting grouches or even cripples, or else turn into healthy, good-natured, long-lasting friends," Pirsig wrote.

I know what Pirsig meant. My first motorcycle, the Harley-Davidson Low Rider, was truly on its way after 50,000 miles to being the "long-lasting friend" Pirsig so eloquently described. I regret having sold it.

At the other end of the spectrum, I owned a used '83 Triumph Bonneville, one of the last out of the factory before the company folded. This "bad-acting grouch," with numerous electrical problems even elicited derisive remarks from mechanics whenever I trucked the bike to the shop for repair. "You know the reason the British drink warm beer is because of the Lucas refrigerators, don't you," remarked a mechanic on one occasion. "The Prince of Darkness," chuckled another.

The LT was showing less than 13,000 miles at the time but I was already pleased about the personality the bike seemed to be developing. One thing seemed clear—the LT is capable of delivering more performance than I am qualified to demand of it. The bike is very, very fast. An "Autobahn Blaster." But it doesn't mock me by broadcasting the difference in the size of our performance envelopes. It's developing the personality of a solid, trustworthy, behind-the-scenes partner—perfectly willing to help me look good and let me take credit for whatever success we may achieve.

As I was confronting my predicament in Florida, murf was having a little excitement on the same highway less than 100 miles to the north, in southern Georgia. A car in front of him on I-95 lost control, and another spun trying to avoid the first one. Fortunately, murf remembered the riding lessons he had taken at Reg Pridmore's world-renowned CLASS course the previous summer. He was able to swerve and control the bike without hitting either the car or falling off his motorcycle. He missed one car by two feet and the other by ten feet.

"You don't get to be a neurosurgeon without having a capacity to learn," murf said later. "Pridmore was standing behind me, whispering in my ear, the whole trip."

Temperamental Trooper
Before I was out of Florida, Martin Hildebrandt was being pulled to the side of the road by a Virginia State Trooper. "I clocked you doing 85 mph. Are you aware that this is forbidden in the U.S.?" asked the officer. "Try to keep the speed down from here on, and remember, this is not the Autobahn."

This wasn't the first time in Martin's trip that an American law enforcement officer reminded him that he wasn't traveling the German Autobahn. His first encounter occurred in Wyoming as he was riding to Salt Lake City from Chicago. He recalled the suggestions that his American friends had made when, before his trip to Salt Lake City, he asked what he should do if stopped for speeding in the United States. "Stop immediately, get off your machine, take off your helmet, have your papers handy, and be very polite," he had been advised.

Although Martin followed the suggestions perfectly, the Wyoming State Trooper stepping from his Dodge Viper had appeared angry. "Are you trying to kill someone with that speeding?"

"No, sir," Martin replied. "I must have forgotten to watch my speedometer for some moments."

"Some moments? I saw you five miles ago and needed all of that distance to catch up! Did you bring $190 in cash?"

"I'm not sure, sir, but I think so," Martin replied.

Actually, Martin left Germany with a $2,000 "ticket budget," but decided it wouldn't be helpful to discuss this with the trooper.

"Sit in my car while we fill out the papers," the trooper snapped.

When Martin seated himself in the ten-cylinder chase vehicle, the trooper pointed to the numerals "115" displayed on the radar unit's read-out. "That's the speed that I clocked you at. Do you know what that means?"

"No sir, not really."

"It means that you're lucky not to be hauled off to jail in handcuffs. If I wrote you a ticket for the speed you were doing, there wouldn't be any question about it. I'm going to write you up for doing 90 mph, but it will cost you a $190 bond."

"Yes sir, thanks very much."

After signing the papers and paying the bond, Martin commented that it surprised him to see a police officer driving an expensive sports car. By now, the trooper's anger seemed to have vanished. "There are only 11 of these in the United States. Keep your speed down a bit if you don't want any trouble. And remember, this is not the Autobahn."

In my experience, state police rarely exhibit anger toward a motorist they have stopped for a violation, unless they have observed reckless behavior or suspect criminal activity. I would expect them to be particularly polite to a visitor from abroad. But when a law enforcement officer must drive over 120 mph to overtake a vehicle, you can bet that the tension elevates his heartbeat and gets his adrenaline flowing.

Fast Food Fright

I usually slow down when I eat on the move. For someone accustomed to higher speeds, 60 mph seems like a crawl, and eating while riding seems like a reasonable thing to do. I paid big bucks for the Shoei "Duo-Tech" helmet because the entire front opens to allow eating or drinking without removing it. I loved this feature. Like most riders, I had also equipped my motorcycle with a throttle lock that enabled me to free my right hand while the motorcycle held the same speed.

I had opened a bag of peanuts and was trying to eat them on the move. I had been riding with the windshield all the way down and was dealing with more wind directly in my face than usual. As I tossed my head back to get some peanuts into my mouth, the wind caught the open face shield and ripped the front assembly all the way to the back of the helmet, shearing the screw securing the right side of the shield to the helmet.

This gave my neck a violent snap and immediately got my adrenaline pumping.

I pulled onto the shoulder of the highway to repair the helmet using the recently purchased duct tape. I don't know how I would have repaired the helmet without the tape. But it ended my eating on the move, as my helmet was now sealed shut.

I arrived in Charleston, South Carolina, at 2:25 p.m. for a bonus gas stop. If I had driven another ten miles or so, I could have collected some bonus points for Savannah as well. I hadn't consulted the atlas recently and wasn't aware that Savannah was so close. That's what sleep deprivation can do.

Damp, Dark, and Deep

A little after 11:00 p.m., I entered the Chesapeake Bay Bridge Tunnel and headed across the dark 17.6-mile expanse of water connecting the Delmarva Peninsula with the Virginia coast. I knew about this engineering marvel, the world's largest bridge-tunnel complex, but had never had the opportunity to see it.

This structure, acclaimed as one of the "Seven Wonders of the Modern World," begins as a bridge where it leaves the mainland at Virginia Beach. A restaurant, gift shop, and fishing pier are located on the southernmost of the four man-made islands. Several miles from shore the highway disappears into a tunnel beneath the ocean. After about a mile, the highway rises to the surface and continues once again as a bridge. All I could see was water—the Chesapeake Bay to one side of the highway and the Atlantic Ocean to the other. After another five miles the highway again descends beneath the ocean and continues through a second tunnel for another mile before rising one final time as a bridge, ending at Cape Charles, Virginia. I enjoyed the crossing and only wished I had been able to make the trip during daylight.

When I stopped at the toll booth at the north end to exchange my $10 fee for a toll receipt, the duct tape prevented me from opening my face shield to offer my customary "thank you" to the attendant. I offered "thumbs up" and a wave instead, recalling the speech veteran Iron Butt rider Gregg Smith had made at the novice rider meeting several evenings ago. Gregg greeted the group with his helmet in place and began his talk to the riders without removing the helmet. After a few sentences, he removed the helmet and continued, "Try to be courteous and think about the image that you are creating about us and about motorcycling. It may be an inconvenience to remove your helmet when you stop to pay for gas, but think about how intimidating it is for you to approach people when they can't see your face. Let's watch out a little for the public image of motorcyclists."

I parked to nap at a rest area within sight of the toll booth. I was exhausted but didn't want to take the time to check into a motel again before reaching Maine. It was close to midnight and the traffic was light. The earplugs blocked the background noise well and I was able to sleep for a few hours.

Peaceful Passage

As I was dozing off, 26-year-old Jesse Pereboom, our youngest rider, was sitting on the bank of the James River less than 75 miles away. Jesse had captured the 379-point bonus for visiting colonial Jamestown, Virginia, but had taken a wrong turn on his way to the Chesapeake Bay Bridge Tunnel. He decided to wait for the ferry rather than take the long ride back to the bridge to cross the river.

It was half past midnight when the ferry left for the opposite bank of the river. Jesse later described the crossing as his most peaceful interlude during the rally. A full moon reflected off the water as Jesse's mind turned back a few centuries and he imagined that he was living in colonial times. He was exhausted and wished the crossing had taken longer, allowing him more time to relax before continuing his journey.

Murf's Monkeyshines

As if the rally itself weren't providing enough of a challenge, the gang's neurosurgeon needed to make the event more interesting. As murf was about to enter the New Jersey Turnpike, he stopped and approached two young state troopers and asked for permission to take their photograph with his pink towel draped across their patrol car. After suggesting that murf was nuts, they refused the request, saying they would be reprimanded by their internal affairs division if the picture were to be published. You would have thought murf had asked the troopers to moon the camera to upstage Rick Morrison's Apollo shot.

Murf got the idea to make this request earlier in the day when he came upon Ed Otto at a roadside park in North Carolina. As they were talking, a North Carolina State Trooper pulled into the rest stop and joined them.

"The trooper, a motorcyclist himself, was more than willing to kick tires and tell lies with us," murf said. "One of the most treasured rally mementos that Ed and I have is a photo of the trooper with our towels draped over the side of his patrol car. I decided to make a game of collecting as many of these pictures as I could during the rest of the rally." Murf abandoned the game after the New Jersey sour-pusses refused to play.

At the same moment, Marty Jones was also on the New Jersey Turnpike, again being pulled to the side of the road by a trooper. Remembering his Texas handcuffing episode, he explained that he was a law enforcement officer *before* mentioning that he was carrying a gun. This worked better. The trooper provided an escort back to the highway and directed him to the shortest route to Connecticut.

Bob Higdon's dispatch for September 5, *Day Seven – Throwing the Dice,* included a discussion of how, when he was in college, he bought a motorcycle to meet women. Later, when he was still young and stupid, he spent six months plotting the fastest way around the country and tried to hit all 48 states in 11 days. He managed that feat in 1987, hitting all the contiguous states in 10.8 days. His report went on to say,

> *The Iron Butt boys and girls—well, the average age of starters was 46.3—are being tempted to do what I did, though the pressures on them are considerably higher. They also have to make checkpoints. I didn't. And I averaged a slothful 750 miles a day. In Florida the bottom man still running was doing better than that, the median rider was averaging 921, and Ron Ayres, at the top, had been hitting 1,150 every day for nearly a week . . .*

Former repeat Iron Butt contestants themselves, Chalmers and Kneebone know that the rally is not won by riding at triple-digit speeds for 23 hours a day. It is a battle between a complex series of bonus trade-offs and a fading capacity to analyze them intelligently. There is normally only one route that will produce a maximum leg score and yet provide at least a minimum amount of rest for the energy to continue. It has never been easy to calculate; this year it's worse.

The Nasty Northeast

When I awoke at the Virginia toll booth area a little after midnight on Tuesday, I remembered that I was about to begin the part of the rally I was looking forward to least—the Mid-Atlantic states and New England. In my opinion, there isn't anything for a motorcyclist to like about this part of the country.

September 1995						
Mon	Tue	Wed	Thur	Fri	Sat	Sun
28	29	30	31	1	2	3
4	5	6	7	8	9	10
11	12	13	14	15	16	17
18	19	20	21	22	23	24
25	26	27	28	29	30	

First, there's the aggravation of having to make frequent stops to pay tolls to use many of the major highways. The stops are more irritating for motorcycles than for other vehicles. Every time the motorcyclist stops to pay a toll, there is a danger of slipping on the residue of oil and grease that cover the center of the lanes where hundreds of vehicles deposited a portion of their crankcase contents.

To avoid applying brakes while the tires are in the center of the lane where sludge accumulates, the rider stays in the left wheel track, which is less slippery. But to shift into neutral to free his hands to pay the toll, the rider must first plant his right foot in the thick of the sludge. And he must remove riding gloves to handle money and to receive and store change and receipts.

In anticipation of the numerous toll booths that I would encounter, I deposited coins and tucked several greenbacks into the zippered pocket on the sleeve of the Aerostich. Andy Goldfine and the boys at Rider Wearhouse did what they could to help riders manage toll-paying chores. Those guys are obviously riders too.

Toll plazas pose the additional hazard of being rear-ended by motorists who misjudge the distance required to stop. Coupled with the heavy traffic, lower speed limits, and poor surface conditions, it isn't hard to see why riders prefer to get New York and New England behind them, preferably at night. Traffic is lighter then, and there isn't anything worth seeing from the highway anyway.

Murf could tell us all something about the crappy roads in this part of the country. As he was circling the nation's capital in the fourth lane of the five-lane beltway, a jarring encounter with a pothole caused his motorcycle to suddenly and unexpectedly stop running. As with my flameout in Jacksonville the previous day, murf's occurred in the middle of heavy traffic. A trucker noticed his plight, understood what was going on, and signaled him to head for the shoulder. The driver used his 18-wheeler to block traffic as murf made his way to the side of the road.

Murf's motorcycle has a sensor to detect if the motorcycle leans too far to the side. The sensor, a pendulum suspended in oil, closes an electrical circuit if the pendulum touches the inner edge of a retaining ring. Theoretically, such an occurrence means the motorcycle has fallen. When the circuit closes, the engine stops running. In murf's case, the shock of hitting the pothole generated enough motion in the device to trigger the shutdown.

The sensor recycles after the ignition switch is turned off and then back on. After determining what had caused the shutdown, murf regained his composure and continued on his way. When murf told me about this, I told him about my episode with a different safety feature. If I ever buy a motorcycle with either feature, I'm going to have them *both* disconnected.

Jerry Clemmons reported meeting Boyd Young on the way to Maine: "I stopped at a rest area near Darlington, Maryland to phone home and saw Boyd Young, one of the Oklahoma riders, pull in as I walked back to my bike. He said he'd been running solid since Ft. Lauderdale and he didn't feel too good.

He looked serious rough to me. I had seen better looking heads on a draft beer."

Ed Otto had arrived in Salisbury, Maryland, several hours ahead of me and had checked into a motel for a two-hour nap. When he tried to sleep through his "Screamin' Meanie" wake-up call, only the pounding from an angry couple in the next room woke him. So he turned off the alarm and went back to sleep. Fortunately for him, he had extracted a promise from the motel clerk to be sure he was up in two hours. When she wasn't able to awaken him with repeated phone calls, she dispatched the security guard to kick him out of bed.

Morris Kruemcke was sitting in a fast food restaurant in Kingsport, Tennessee, more than 400 miles to the west. He had just added two more notches to his 48-state belt: Kentucky and Tennessee. He pulled out his HP palmtop computer to do a quick check on his progress and quickly determined he would have to hurry to make it to Gorham in time to avoid penalties. He could make it all the way to Gorham without leaving the interstate highway system, but he still had nearly 950 miles to cover in less than half a day.

It was only 5:30 a.m. when I stopped in Dover, Delaware, for gas, but the tempo of commuter traffic into Philadelphia/New Jersey/New York was already starting to build. I pressed on, unhappy that my timing would put me in New York during morning traffic. I arrived in West Haven, Connecticut, by about 11:30 a.m. and made the mistake of stopping for gas. A bonus was available for purchasing gas in New Haven, a few blocks farther. I caught the mistake before the tank was full and bought gas twice in five minutes. Chalmers had warned us that if the bonus called for a purchase in a particular city, only that specific city's name on the receipt would count.

I didn't know it at the time, but Boyd Young and I had been within a few miles of each other on I-95 as we approached the George Washington Bridge. Boyd was ahead of me, about to cross into the Bronx, when he heard a loud explosion as a large dump truck directly in front of him listed hard to one side. A large fragment of rubber from the truck's blown tire slammed into Boyd's windshield, and another glanced off his helmet. Fortunately, he was fine.

Depressing, Devastating DNF

Fritz and Phyllis Lang, who had been time-barred in Florida, arrived in the Baltimore/Washington area and realized that they wouldn't make it to Maine in time for that checkpoint, either. Their ride through the tail end of the hurricane had taken too much out of them. They wouldn't be able to qualify as finishers, as the rules allow being time-barred at only one checkpoint. They were bitterly disappointed by the prospect of their second Iron Butt DNF—The Langs are such committed motorcycle enthusiasts that they don't own an automobile and they ride to work all year.

Phyllis couldn't help crying. She didn't want to go home, but she didn't want to return to Salt Lake City and face the other riders in defeat, either. She and Fritz opted instead for the Blue Ridge Parkway and spent a few days in Boone, North Carolina. They took little comfort from knowing they had already accomplished more than most motorcyclists ever would.

Practicing Prudence

In light of losing my receipts on the transcontinental leg and nearly being time-barred in Ft. Lauderdale, I didn't want to overextend myself on the way to Maine. I only went after the bonuses along my direct route. My only side trip was to Beaver Tail Park on Conanicut Island, at the entrance to Rhode Island's Narragansett Bay.

I'm less familiar with New England than I am with most other areas of the United States. Despite my negative feelings about the toll roads in the region, I welcomed the opportunity to expand my New England experience with the Rhode Island bonus stop. It was a beautiful day and I had plenty of daylight. Like Laughlin, Nevada, Conanicut Island was a pleasant surprise and made it to my short list of locations to which I'd like to return with Barb for a long weekend.

The first Beavertail Lighthouse, a wooden tower built in 1749, was America's third lighthouse. The tower was set on fire by the British as they left the area at the end of the American Revolution, but it was repaired and remained in service until 1854. Although a museum is maintained in the keeper's house, I limited my visit to the required photo of the visitor sign.

My trip to the island was one of the few times I met another Iron Butt rider. Jesse Pereboom had pulled up to the visitor sign at the park entrance on his blue Harley Electraglide as I was going through my exit routine. Jesse and Martin Hildebrandt were the only entrants under the age of 30. And Jesse, at 26, would be the youngest rider to ever finish an Iron Butt, if he could make it to Salt Lake City by 5:00 p.m. on Saturday. Someone had commented that Jesse was younger than Bob Honemann's BMW and Leonard Aron's Indian Chief. Both motorcycles were now out of it, but Jesse was still going.

A year before the rally, Jesse had written to the 1995 entrants and invited them to meet him in Sturgis, South Dakota, at The Broken Spoke Saloon, offering to buy a drink for any rider who could make it.

Only 5,000 people live in Sturgis, but once a year, in the first week of August, nearly a quarter-million bikers and tourists pour into this small town near Mount Rushmore to attend the mother of all motorcycle gatherings, the Black Hills Classic.

Jesse assumed that many riders would meet him at the "World's Most Famous Biker Bar." The Broken Spoke is so biker-oriented that when it first opened in 1987, customers could bring their motorcycles right up to the bar for a drink. Jesse's invitation was a great idea, but Suzy Johnson was the only rider to visit the saloon to accept the offer.

Jesse is from Webster, a small South Dakota town almost 400 miles from Sturgis, in the northeastern part of the state. Until shortly before the rally, Jesse managed the family-owned business, Pereboom's Café, with his brothers. Jesse was in the process of moving to Glendale, Arizona, to learn to be a motorcycle mechanic when the Iron Butt was held. Jesse and I chatted for a minute or two before I left for Gorham. Once again, I felt a mild tinge of guilt for leaving abruptly and not offering to ride together.

Lunching on Lobster

As I left the island and passed several charming little seaside restaurants, Martin Hildebrandt was sitting at a restaurant in Portland, Maine eating *several* Maine lobsters. He had arrived at the checkpoint nearly eight hours early, with no other riders in sight. He questioned the staff to ensure that he hadn't missed a state called Providence. When reassured one more time, he asked for directions to a restaurant where he could try some of the Maine lobster that he had heard so much about.

"A nice lady working at the shop encouraged me to get some sleep, after riding so far. My tired brain cells told me that she was right, but in spite of my sore knee and ankle that were pressed between the semi and the mobile home so many hours ago, I really felt very good. I was exhausted, but in a strange way felt good anyway. I felt so damn well in fact that I imagined that I must feel better than at any other time during the rally. And this area reminded me of home. A peaceful, clean and cool late summer morning in the forest. It was so beautiful that I had to resist crying.

"I had promised myself some lobster if I made it to Maine. The staff at the shop thought I was crazy, but directed me to a good seafood restaurant in Portland anyway. This was the most beautiful day in the world and I had a lot of time left. So I took a pleasant 20-minute ride to the restaurant, parked the motorcycle, and walked inside. A nice girl at the counter asked me to take my choice from the living lobsters in the tank. I selected three. After making sure that she really understood what I meant, she apparently decided that I was a mad tourist like the others and gave me what I had requested.

"A few minutes later I felt that I was sitting at Scarborough Fair with some of the best food on earth. I slipped into a deep and overwhelming peace. All stress, pain, and problems were gone. All that remained was quiet peace. I thought about how nice it would have been to sit here with my friend Leonard and chat about old and new friends and old and new worlds. I committed to talk him into coming here someday. I know he missed the Florida checkpoint, but I hoped that somehow he would be able to make Maine nonetheless.

"Leonard is a fighter and somehow I expected him to turn round the corner at any moment. So as I left the restaurant, I asked the girl to give Leonard my greetings in case he should show up. She didn't believe a word of what I said, but she didn't want to argue with a big smelly foreigner in black leathers. Somehow I was convinced he would receive my message. He would ask for the best place to go. I was sure about that."

Frenzy in the Forest

Jerry Clemmons made the Maine checkpoint with two and a half hours to spare. It had been a weak leg for Jerry, and after weaving his way through all of the traffic in the New York and New England area, he was totally beaten. "I was just glad to be alive," he told me later. "Someone was interviewing us with a camera and microphone, but they broke away when Garve Nelson arrived on his Honda Ascot. He was a star. Everyone wanted to see 'the old guy.' So I quit talking, as my audience departed and there was no longer anyone around to listen."

"The checkpoint was real noisy, as there were a lot of spectators in addition to the TV people. Tom Loegering was on the ground, sleeping through all this racket. I was beginning to think one of the differences between the Big Dogs and the also-rans like me might be their ability to drop and sleep in a bed of rocks and briars, with an Aerostich suit and helmet still on, a crowd of noisy people standing all around them, and strobe lights glowing and cameras rolling. I faked sleeping at Salt Lake and Spokane with all the commotion going on, but gave it up by the time we reached San Diego."

As I entered Maine, I noticed that the leaves were beginning to turn color. And this was only the first week of September. I knew that in the next several weeks the region would change to dazzling shades of red, yellow, and orange. Motorcyclists would once again be wary of slipping on moist leaves covering the roads.

I passed a BMW automobile and the passengers began waving, trying to attract my attention. I always return waves, but they usually come from children rather than adults. I assumed that either they were impressed that both of our vehicles were from Bavaria or that they had been drinking. They were having too much fun. I always get cautious when I'm around drivers I suspect of drinking.

When I exited the turnpike, the BMW remained behind me, and I tried to remain cautious. The car was following at a safe distance. As I approached the Reynolds Sportcenter checkpoint in Gorham, I realized that the occupants of the car were on their way to visit the riders and to cheer them on.

Gorham is a rural town about fifteen miles west of Portland. I arrived shortly before 6:00 p.m., the scheduled opening. This was the first checkpoint I made without losing any points for a late arrival. Things seemed a lot more frenzied than at previous checkpoints, and the rally workers couldn't check me in right away. Although I was tired and cranky, I resisted any urge to become impatient with these volunteers. I recalled Steve Chalmers emphasizing that being impolite to rally workers would result in disqualification. Besides, being impolite would have bothered my conscience and I didn't need any additional mental burdens.

Reynolds Sportcenter provided excellent service. The service area was bustling with riders in line for tire changes and service. The worker in the parts department repaired my helmet and refused payment. What a relief to know I could once again eat and drink without having to remove my helmet. The service department changed the oil and repaired my broken luggage rack, charging me only for the oil.

Ron Major had shipped replacement tires to Gorham prior to the rally, but decided to forgo the tire change and instead shipped the tires home.

"Just goes to show you how conservatively I've been riding this time," Ron crowed. "Last time my rear tire was totally shot when I arrived here. This year I've got more miles on it than last time and still have enough tread left to get back home."

I spoke with Ron about his accident the last time he was in Gorham. During the 1993 rally, a car pulled in front of him as he was leaving. He had the right-of-way at a "T" intersection, and hit the small car broadside. Ron suffered a number of broken bones, was knocked unconscious, and was hospitalized.

The accident totaled both vehicles. He reported having been overcome with a very eerie feeling as he entered Gorham and passed the intersection where he nearly died two years earlier. "I slowed down and studied the location as I passed," Ron reported. "God, what a strange feeling. This was the first time I saw the location since my accident."

"Think I'll trade a half-hour nap for the tire change," he remarked as he looked for a place to lie down.

Returning to the checkpoint after his lobster feast, Martin Hildebrandt met other arriving riders and decided he had enough time to attempt to repair his GPS system for the third time. The unit had been on the blink since Los Angeles. Martin was able to talk Keith Keating into making a trip to a Radio Shack for parts.

Martin wasn't in last place in Maine, but he wasn't far from it. This was misleading, since any rider who managed to earn the 3,000-point bonus for visiting all 48 states wouldn't have those points reflected in his score until the end of the rally. Considering what other riders had been through, Martin was in relatively good shape. He didn't seem to care about his standing. He hardly glanced at the bonus sheets as they were distributed. He was just pleased that he had his computer working again and had programmed a route that would enable him to claim the 48-state bonus.

Showing the Strain

Riders were really haggard and hollow-eyed now, and their judgment was more impaired than ever. Karol Patzer was a little frazzled after arriving more than an hour after the Gorham window opened. This was her first checkpoint that resulted in a penalty assessment. She vowed to be a lot more careful in returning to Salt Lake City.

Jerry Clemmons related an incident that revealed their tired state of mind. Before going to the restroom, Karol asked Jerry to hold her purse. He later thought this had been a strange request because the restroom was large enough to accommodate both Karol and her purse. And he felt that it reflected on his own judgment because, in spite of his manhood, he agreed to hold it.

Shortly before standings were announced, I saw Eddie Metz and asked how he was doing. He was dejected and talked of "chucking it" if he wasn't in the top ten. He had been feeling flu-like symptoms since he was caught in the heavy rain in Florida and he was complaining that his knees were sore. If he had lost his bonus receipts as I had, he said, he would have headed for home.

Eddie's remarks were indicative of the attitude of many riders at this stage. It would only get worse. At this point, many riders wanted only to finish and didn't care about additional bonuses. Fourteen riders had already been eliminated from the rally. This leg would take a heavy toll. We all expected the concluding leg to be a real son-of-a-bitch.

STANDINGS IN GORHAM

Standing	Rider	Motorcycle	Points
1	Eddie James	'93 BMW K1100RS	13,669
2	Marty Jones	'92 Kawasaki Voyager	13,652
3	Tom Loegering	'95 BMW R1100GS	13,263
4	Gary Eagan	'94 BMW K1100LT	12,982
5	Ron Ayres	'95 BMW K1100LT	12,966
6	Eddie Metz	'85 Honda Gold Wing	12,791
7	Eugene McKinney	'94 BMR R1100RS	12,763
8	Jesse Pereboom	'93 Harley-Davidson FLHT	12,746
9	Ron Major	'94 Honda ST1100	12,727
10	Roy Eastwood	'94 BMW R1100RS	12,476

Shuffled Standings

The Maine checkpoint saw significant movement in rider standings and gave us our first glimpse of likely finishing positions. Eddie James was now in first place and Eddie Metz, who was delighted in Ft. Lauderdale when he saw his name listed in second place, found that he had slipped to sixth.

An excerpt of Bob Higdon's Internet installment, *Day Eight – Iron Men, Iron Butts, and Iron Bears,* mentioned Eddie James and Lyle:

The BMW K1100RS aimed by the stuffed bear, Lyle, with
Eddie James riding along for comic relief, jumped from
fourth to first place at the Gorham, Maine checkpoint today.
This raunchy animal, tattered beyond human powers of
description, moth-eaten and patched, and looking as if it is
something that a cat wouldn't even want to bring in the
house, has ridden steadily from the start. The stuffed bear is
having a good ride too.

Tom Loegering, remarkably, rose from fifteenth to third place, the first time his name appeared with the Big Dogs. Tom reported that he was feeling great, had a lot of energy flowing, and was able to gather a lot of bonus points on his ride north from Florida. His accomplishments included a trip to the tip of Cape Cod, right in the midst of Labor Day traffic.

While discussing his accomplishment with his fellow riders in Gorham, Tom referred to the Cape Cod bonus as a "sucker bet," like the Golden Gate Bridge and Mount Rushmore. He claimed he could have captured more points by doing less riding to the Fort Kent bonus in northern Maine.

Actually, Fort Kent would have added 345 more points to his total, but it would have been at the expense of a much longer trip. Assuming that he came up I-95 through the Boston area, the trip to Gorham via Fort Kent rather than Cape Cod would have added 350 miles to his total distance traveled. Even if he had come north via the giant bonus in Buffalo, New York, the trip to Fort Kent would have increased the distance by at least 170 miles and would also have meant losing time crossing into Canada and back into the United States.

Local Legend Lags
The standings at the first three checkpoints didn't have much in common except that Gary Eagan was always in first place. The Florida-to-Maine leg saw him drop to fourth place after bypassing a 278-point bonus in North Carolina and then experiencing problems with his motorcycle. When he couldn't find the Biltmore Mansion in the Blue Ridge Mountains near Asheville, North Carolina, he decided to continue north, rather than invest more time in the search.

Tom Loegering, Sr. and Roy Eastwood hopped into the top ten on leg four. Here they are before the rally, pictured with other BMW R-bike riders; left to right: Eugene McKinney, Hank Rowland, Loegering, Keith Keating, Rick Morrison, Eastwood, Rick Shrader, and Bob Honemann.

After reaching Middlesboro, Kentucky, his motorcycle started to backfire, then made a sickening clanging sound. Gary, who admits to having no mechanical aptitude whatsoever, pulled into a gasoline station and asked for advice from the attendant. The attendant suggested that the problem was caused by a rod or valve and that Gary was "about to toast the puppy."

After snatching a sizable bonus in Bluefield, West Virginia, the noise from his motorcycle got so bad that he believed the engine was about to seize. He decided to bypass other bonuses in the eastern corridor and instead headed directly for Maine at 65 mph with one hand covering the clutch lever to disengage the engine if it froze. He passed stops in Delaware and New Jersey, ending his attempt to collect the big 48-state bonus. He thought that with luck he could have repairs made and at least finish the rally. He had written off all hope of winning.

When he arrived in Gorham, a number of people listened to the bike but offered no help. It was the consensus of those who listened to it that the bike was shot. "I had a good ride going, and it's too bad it has to end like this, but that's the Butt," he thought.

Then Boyd Young listened to the bike and suggested the exhaust bolts may have backed out and required tightening. He showed Gary where to tighten and told him what size socket to use. That solved the problem. Gary was prepared to resume his original pace, but the diversion from his original plan had already cost him the 3,000-point bonus for visiting the contiguous states and other lost bonuses.

Jesse Pereboom made it to number eight, the highest standing any of the Harley pilots attained during the rally. But the effort came at great expense. Jesse was bruised by the beating he had given himself between Florida and Maine. He decided to get a full night's sleep before tackling the fifth and final leg back to Salt Lake City.

Rick Morrison overslept at a rest area in Virginia and didn't make it to the Maine checkpoint before it closed. This drove him from top ten status to thirty-ninth position. Suzy Johnson and Chuck Pickett also missed the Maine checkpoint, but all three riders continued running in hopes of visiting Gorham and returning to Salt Lake City in time to avoid the dreaded DNF.

I was elated to learn that I had climbed two places in the standings and was now fifth, despite the loss of bonus credits in Texas and the penalty for being late in Ft. Lauderdale. I felt I had an opportunity to finish in the top three. But the most arduous leg of the Rally still awaited me. The final packet of bonuses was distributed promptly at 8:00 p.m.

I hadn't been to a motel since Ft. Lauderdale. I couldn't resist peeking at the remaining obstacles that the bonuses of the final leg would impose. I glanced at the list to determine what would be required to claim the largest ones.

Opportunities or Obstacles?

I didn't need Automap Pro to discount the 2,485-point bonus that riding to Salt Lake City via Blaine, Washington, would entail. That trip would require three 1,300-mile days, back to back. I had never done anything like it and didn't intend to tackle it after the exertion of the previous eight days. I also discounted the next largest bonus in Venice, Louisiana. I didn't like the idea of having to travel secondary roads to get there.

The next two large bonuses, Mackinaw City in northern Michigan and the Freshwater Fisherman Hall of Fame in Wisconsin's north woods, were more appealing. I always wanted to ride in the UP (Michigan's Upper Peninsula) along the northern shore of Lake Michigan. I also welcomed the opportunity to end the rally riding the northern route through the sparsely populated Dakotas, Montana, and Wyoming. The route would take me over the Mackinaw Bridge, one of the world's longest suspension bridges, which connects Mackinaw City in the south and St. Ignace in the north.

The Lafayette and Dover, Tennessee, bonus had an interesting twist, as it was necessary to visit both locations to earn the points. At this point in the rally, many tired riders would overlook such nuances.

Only one shot remained on my Polaroid flashbar and I knew it would be dark when I got to the UP. Before looking for a motel, I tried to buy another flashbar at a local Kmart, but no luck. I had unintentionally violated a cardinal rule of endurance rallies: buy everything you need before starting. The rally leaves no time for shopping.

After disappointment at the Kmart, I decided to risk the long ride to the UP with only one shot at getting the required photo in Mackinaw City. I could claim the bonus points by buying gas, but the rally packet warned that the gas station in the town wouldn't be open when I planned to arrive.

I located a suitable motel, checked in, and lugged my gear into the room. Although I decided to get some sleep before leaving Maine, other riders, apparently more rested than I, were eager to get after some of the big bonuses on this final leg of the rally. Boyd Young, who admits that he felt like crying after blowing the previous leg and dropping from eighth place in Florida to nineteenth in Maine, was eager to recapture a "top ten" position. As he was reviewing the list of obstacles, he overheard Eddie James comment on one of them.

"Oh, the Newport Toll Bridge. I know exactly where that is," Eddie remarked. "It's just 200 miles south of here."

Until he heard Eddie's comment, Boyd was intending to plan the final leg before leaving the checkpoint. He decided instead to follow Eddie to the first bonus and plan the rest of the leg afterward. As the two riders were approaching the Rhode Island state line in pursuit of the 291-point bonus, Boyd's heart sank as a Massachusetts State Trooper began conducting a pursuit of his own. Boyd saw the traditional light show that suggested it was time to pull over for a conversation about Boyd's elevated and aggressive riding style.

As Boyd stopped to take his medicine, the trooper decided instead to pull back onto the highway to pursue Eddie and Lyle the Bear, who had been riding a few car lengths ahead in the far left lane. Boyd sat on the shoulder of the highway within sight of an exit ramp leading to a service station. After a few minutes, he rode down the shoulder of the road, made his way up the ramp, and pulled into the service station. He prolonged his stay before continuing to Newport.

While Boyd was sitting at the service station, Eddie was explaining to the trooper that he and Lyle were on their way to a "charity run" and that he didn't want to be late. The trooper gave James a verbal warning, saying "I can't give a ticket to a man with a teddy bear."

**Leg 5 – Gorham to Salt Lake City,
Author's Route**

7

Gorham to Salt Lake City

2,436 miles – 72 hours

Heading Home

I left Gorham about midnight Wednesday after a four-hour nap and headed south on I-95. Gary Eagan was already on his way to the bonuses in Mackinaw City and Hayward, Wisconsin. He had opted for the most direct route available, through Canada.

September 1995						
Mon	Tue	Wed	Thur	Fri	Sat	Sun
28	29	30	31	1	2	3
4	5	6	7	8	9	10
11	12	13	14	15	16	17
18	19	20	21	22	23	24
25	26	27	28	29	30	

I had briefly considered the Canadian route to Mackinaw City but discounted the idea. I suspected I might have to show proof of Canadian motorcycle insurance, which I didn't have. Also, I was laboring under the misconception that radar detectors were illegal in Canada and that perhaps I wouldn't make it through immigration with mine. Besides, I was unfamiliar with the penalties for speeding in Canada. I decided to take a longer route, staying in the U.S.

Morris Kruemcke was heading for the toll bridge at New-port, Rhode Island, to collect his first 291 bonus points out of Gorham. He would later describe the 200-mile detour from his prior plan as the fatal mistake that cost him the 48-state bonus and a few places in the final standings. Until he made the decision to go for this bonus, he thought he was on track to make all of the states. But the trip to Newport delayed him suffi-ciently that he soon realized that he would have to abandon the 48-state quest.

It wasn't long after the Maine checkpoint that Jerry Clem-mons abandoned the 225-point gas log bonus for the last leg. "I was very tired when my fuel started running low, so I wasn't thinking real clearly. I pulled into an independent gas station, where I had no credit card. I was 50 miles down the road when I realized that I hadn't collected my gas receipt. This is where I made the decision not to have the 225-point gas log bonus on this leg."

Pondering the Perils

As I was negotiating the narrow two-lane roads leaving Gorham, I thought again about the serious accident that Ron Major had suffered here during the 1993 rally. Although no rider has yet died or become permanently disabled as a result of injuries sustained in an Iron Butt, nearly every rally has had its accidents, though usually not involving other vehicles. The most common rally accidents result from "deer strikes" or from riders running off the road after falling asleep or otherwise suffering the effects of fatigue.

Ron Major wasn't the only rider injured in the 1993 Iron Butt. Marty Jones totaled his motorcycle and broke his leg in the process. And riders were aware of how Rick Shrader earned the moniker "Swamp Thing" in the 1991 Iron Butt. Harold Brooks and Dave McQueeny had serious accidents in that rally as well. This year Ciccarelli and Attwood were out of action as a result of deer strikes and Kellerman ran off the road, appar-ently after falling asleep. And Losofsky was out after having his leg injured by a stone thrown by a truck in Utah.

Experienced riders wouldn't argue that participation in the Iron Butt is the safest way to spend 11 days. Bob Higdon wrote a column once that described how he invested considerable time studying mountains of data about motorcycle accidents. He came away from the project describing riding a motorcycle as the best way to ensure that you won't safely make it from point A to point B. Despite such studies, I *almost* always feel safe, in total control, and capable of avoiding all but the most freakish accident. But I have such an appreciation for potential dangers that I never encourage others to participate. Only experienced riders who are compelled to do this should even consider it.

Several times I found myself hoping to not learn about the loss of a rider to a fatal accident. I knew that even if a rider were killed during the rally, the event would go on. It's a gruesome thought, but considering the duration of the rally, it's conceivable that funeral services for a rider who had died could be over before the end of the rally.

I sometimes wondered if the loss of a rider would keep me from riding. Would I take such an occurrence as an omen to stop? Was there a lesson in Suzy Johnson's experience? She took up motorcycling two years after her son-in-law died in a motorcycle accident. Dave had attended a Harley rally on a Saturday afternoon and headed home on his motorcycle after drinking and partying. He was only two miles from his home when he ran into a telephone pole while trying to negotiate a curve. It was unlikely that he ever knew what he had hit. He died two days later, eight seconds after the doctors unplugged his life support.

Dave and his wife, Tisa, Suzy's daughter, already had two sons under three years old, and Tisa was two months pregnant. Suzy still doesn't know how Tisa avoided losing the baby. She is now a single mother, recently became a teacher, and is still bitter about losing her husband—she blames Dave's Harley and friends as much as his drinking, Suzy told me.

Two years after Dave's death, Suzy went to Sturgis, took a ride on a Moto Guzzi, and became hooked. She bought her first motorcycle a month after she returned home, and didn't tell her daughter. Suzy's ex-fiancée did. When Tisa found out, she wanted to have her mother committed. Before Dave's death,

Suzy never had any desire to ride a motorcycle. She now insists that Dave is haunting her and believes that he and her other friends up there ride with her everywhere she goes.

I've thought a lot about the perils of endurance riding and am prepared to accept the dangers, but I also contend that a rider can do a lot to mitigate the risks.

First, the majority of motorcycle accidents occur at intersections, as with Ron Major's accident in Gorham. A disproportionate number of accidents involve motorcyclists who don't have formal training and, often, not even a motorcycle endorsement on their driver's license. And a disproportionate number of fatalities involve the use of alcohol.

I never drink before riding, and unless I'm on a rally I avoid being out between Saturday evening and Sunday morning, when, according to some studies, more than half of the drivers on the road are legally drunk. I have had advanced rider training, always wear my protective riding suit and other gear, and concentrate on being alert near intersections. During rallies like the Iron Butt, a lot of riding occurs on interstate highways where intersections aren't a problem. The greatest danger is continuing to ride when fatigued.

I have never encouraged my sons to participate in this sport. Although all three of them have motorcycle endorsements on their licenses and have received motorcycle training, I feel fortunate that they haven't shown an interest in following me into this obsession.

Often, between rallies, I question if I should continue to participate in them, considering the dangers. When anticipating a coming rally, I sometimes feel a twinge of trepidation, knowing that I may be putting myself in harm's way. But when I get on the motorcycle I feel totally comfortable, even in heavy traffic. If anything, I battle a tendency to feel invulnerable when I'm on the motorcycle.

There are two situations in which I don't feel comfortable: when I'm passing an 18-wheeler at high speed in a heavy rain, particularly if the wind is also heavy, and when negotiating downhill "sweepers" in the mountains in the midst of a convoy of trucks. Because of the curves, it isn't safe to overtake them too quickly due to the high speeds required to do so. Although it may be my imagination, I often feel that there is a lot of testosterone at work, with truckers trying to prove their trucks are as nimble on mountain roads as my motorcycle is.

You must pass the trucks, otherwise left lane traffic attempting to pass will be on your tail. Riding slower in the right lane isn't a desirable option because trucks will ride your tail all the way down the mountain, threatening to run over you. The only choice is to get in the left lane and pass as quickly as you safely can. This often results in riding closely beside them through sharp curves at high speed.

The apprehension that I feel at such times is primarily from distrusting the truckers. Most are competent, but some probably don't give a damn or are tired, drunk, or drugged. I understand that the drivers are professionals and are less of a threat than John Q. Public in the family sedan. But trucks are more intimidating because of their size.

Foolishly Fretting

I made my way to Detroit via Framingham, Albany, Warner's, Angola, and Westlake, Ohio. At a gas stop on the New York Turnpike, the attendant expressed interest in my trip, and seemed knowledgeable about the bridge crossing at Mackinaw City. He gave me cause for concern when he informed me that motorcycles aren't always allowed to cross, particularly unescorted, because of high winds sometimes encountered on the bridge.

When asked specifically what could happen, he replied: "You could be blown over the side. Even large trucks are sometimes prohibited from crossing without a police escort." I would have ignored his warning if he hadn't sounded so credible. He gave me something new to worry about.

What if I invested all those miles in getting to the bridge only to find that I wouldn't be permitted to cross? What if there were high winds and they simply said, "Cross at your own risk?" Surely there were guard rails to keep me and the motorcycle from being blown into the water. What if they aren't high enough? How could I survive the long fall to the water after being blown from the bridge in helmet, riding suit, heavy boots, and a lot of clothing? Disrobing is difficult enough above water.

After so long on the road and being a bit tired, I began to have thoughts that seemed reasonable then, but in retrospect seem preposterous. I tried to plan for disaster. If the situation appeared dangerous, I thought, I would proceed but would first undo the strap to my helmet until I got to the other side. I would also undo the zippers to my riding boots so that I could get rid of them easily if I found myself in the water. I would only have to work my way out of the suit and work my way to the surface. I even tried to recall the rules for water survival that I learned as a Boy Scout more than 30 years ago.

Not all riders took this northern route. Shortly after Spirit Harley-Davidson opened its doors for business, Jerry Clemmons walked in to earn 486 points for having his paperwork signed. The dealership is about four miles from Pittsburgh, and many riders reported difficulty finding it.

The owner of the shop treated Jerry like royalty and introduced him to his early morning customers. "This fellow is one of those Iron Butt guys," the dealer beamed. "He has to make 1,000 miles a day." Jerry appreciated the recognition.

"Son, you look pretty bad," the dealer continued. "Looks like you could use a little of the bean." He served Jerry some hot coffee and an egg sandwich.

Monitored by Mother Michael

When Boyd entered the shop a little later, Jerry was already on his way, but Eddie James was waiting the 20 minutes necessary to claim the bonus points. Boyd discovered that he and Eddie had crossed the toll bridge at Newport at midnight, within two minutes of each other. They'd lost track of each other when Eddie was stopped by the Massachusetts State Trooper.

The phone rang while Boyd was waiting to have his paperwork signed. The phone call was for him. Boyd was surprised when he took the receiver and found it was Mike Kneebone on the line, inquiring about his progress. When I learned of the call, I thought once again about my fantasy tracking system and about how Mike may have employed it to keep tabs on his riders.

Tom Loegering also visited Spirit Harley-Davidson. Tom not only had difficulty finding the shop, he also became lost after leaving it. He became more lost than at any other time during the rally. When he asked a motorist for directions, the driver took pity on him and led him to his destination in Ohio via back roads that Tom would not have been able to find on his own.

A few hours after entering Ohio, Tom realized that all the receipts he had accumulated since the Maine checkpoint had blown away because he failed to zip the Aerostich pocket in which he had been storing them. Following the example set by the Langs, Chuck Pickett, and me, Tom contributed to the establishment of a fascinating pattern of illogical behavior that would amuse and amaze during gatherings of riders in the coming years. Like Fritz Lang, Tom was successful in retrieving his lost receipts, but he lost more than three hours doing it.

Charles Elberfeld also selected a more southerly route to Salt Lake City than Eagan and I had. In the late afternoon, Charles stopped at his home near Cleveland, surprising his wife and family. During a three-hour stop, he managed to take a bath and grab a quick nap before getting on the road again. Apparently, Charles was able to escape the "stopping-at-home" trap. We lost Kevin Mello to this malady when he stopped at home in Massachusetts on his way to Maine and wasn't heard from again.

While Charles was napping at home, Jerry Clemmons was frantically searching for the motorcycle museum bonus location in Westerville, Ohio. With the help of a motorist at a traffic light, Jerry was able to get directions and made it to the museum as it was about to close. He bought a trinket at the gift shop and hurried to the motorcycle to continue his trip west.

When Jerry reached Indianapolis, he knew it was time to take another motel room to grab some sleep. He was so fatigued that he neglected to put the side stand to the motorcycle down as he attempted to park it. The motorcycle crashed to the pavement. He didn't know whether to be happy that there were people watching who could help him lift the heavy Gold Wing, or embarrassed that others were witness to his sleep-deprived condition.

Bob Higdon's summary for the day, *Day Nine – Out of Sight—Out of Their Minds,* reflected the fatigue that was being felt by other riders too:

> *For nine days they have been on the road in a contest that has taxed them close to their considerable limits. As exhaustion sets in, they are beginning to make rookie mistakes, jeopardizing their chances ever to finish.*
>
> *Steady Eddie Metz went to one bonus in West Virginia but didn't do two others in the vicinity. Gary Eagan nailed 14 states on the road north, but inexplicably missed New Jersey and Delaware. Morris Kruemcke did the same thing. Are these riders, who have left most of the field in their wake, fading, or are they simply trying to lull their competitors into a false sense of security? No one knows.*

Bob had no way of knowing about the difficulties that Gary had experienced with his motorcycle between Florida and Maine. But after dealing with the loose exhaust bolts in Gorham, Gary had resumed a winning pace. He took the direct route through Canada, requiring him to ride 130 fewer miles than I rode to get from Gorham to Mackinaw City. Though he didn't have to drive through Detroit, he experienced snow, sleet and rain during the Canadian portion of his ride.

Depressed by Detroit

As I approached Detroit at sundown, I needed gas and wanted to don an additional pair of long underwear. I pulled into a gasoline station, but there was no rest room, and the clerk was in a bulletproof cage. The precautions seemed appropriate to the neighborhood and clientele.

I had carried my extra clothes inside, but was relieved that there was nowhere to change, because I was having second thoughts about leaving the motorcycle unattended. This was the only time during the trip that I was uneasy about it being left unattended, or concerned about my personal safety.

I bought gas and got back on I-75, looking over my shoulder the entire time. I continued north on I-75 in cold heavy rain until I left the suburbs of Detroit. I wondered how many other riders had decided to tackle the Mackinaw City and Hayward bonuses. I wondered how many of the riders were ahead of me and how many were behind. I also wondered if others had experienced the rain that was now drenching me.

Freezing when I came upon the first rest area in the boondocks beyond the Detroit metropolitan area, I decided to stop. In Florida, rest stops had security guards after dark. Security was required to counteract the negative publicity associated with the murder of foreign tourists at rest stops. Virginia simply closed rest areas at night. While turning onto the exit ramp, I wondered about the policy in Michigan, particularly as I was within about an hour's drive from Detroit.

It would take me a while to enter the men's room and peel through several layers to reach the thermal underwear at the bottom and build back up, all this while the motorcycle would be unattended. There was no sign of anyone. Semis were parked, but I didn't count on them for security, as I assumed the drivers were asleep. As I entered the dark parking area, motion detectors activated bright lights. The overhead mercury vapor lamps flooded the area in light. Very comforting. I parked the motorcycle, took my clothes, and walked into the men's room to change. I carried the Aerostich from the restroom back to the parking lot to minimize the time spent out of sight of the motorcycle.

While finishing my dressing in the parking lot, a friendly Michigan State Trooper pulled up beside the motorcycle, rolled down her window, and engaged me in conversation. "Getting suited up for winter?" she asked.

The Aerostich resembles the snow suits that snowmobilers use in these northern climes. She was interested in what I was doing. When I told her I was headed for Mackinaw City, she quipped that they probably had last winter's ice cleared from the water by then. Considering the remarks made at the gas stop earlier in the day about the problems in crossing the bridge, I considered asking if she was aware of any problems with the intended route. I decided it wouldn't help my macho image—after all, she was a state trooper. Besides, I had given her the opening to say, "Surely you aren't planning to cross the bridge up there on a motorcycle?" She offered no such remark, so I didn't bring up the subject. She waited five minutes or so, until I was ready to push on, and wished me well.

I worried about being able to find gas in the middle of the night in this heavily forested and sparsely populated area. A clerk at the next gas stop put my mind at ease, saying that all of the Shell stations in the Michigan's Upper Peninsula are open 24 hours. "When you're about to enter an area where gas isn't available for 100 miles or so, you'll see a warning sign," he said.

I didn't worry about it any more, but don't remember seeing any warning signs. I tried to make it a point to mention to all gas attendants that I was heading for the bridge at Mackinaw City, giving all of them the opportunity to offer advice. No one did.

Bridging the Barrier

On arriving at Mackinaw City, a bit past midnight on Thursday, I was low on gas and looked for an open station. To qualify for the bonus, I needed either a gas receipt or a photo of the city limit sign. Because I only had one flash left, I wanted to pre-

September 1995						
Mon	Tue	Wed	Thur	Fri	Sat	Sun
28	29	30	31	1	2	3
4	5	6	7	8	9	10
11	12	13	14	15	16	17
18	19	20	21	22	23	24
25	26	27	28	29	30	

serve it if possible. All stations were closed, so I stopped at a motel for directions. The clerk informed me that the next gas available was across the bridge, which wouldn't give me the needed bonus receipt.

I returned to the city limit sign to take the shot for the 701-point bonus. I was careful to set up the shot properly. Chalmers had warned us that if the towel wasn't clearly visible, the photo would be worthless. The picture turned out fine and I headed for the bridge.

My bridge concerns returned when I saw large signs announcing that trucks must stop to determine if escorts were necessary. My last hope was that if the crossing was dangerous, the agent at the toll booth wouldn't permit me to proceed. No comment from the attendant.

"Looks a bit windy up there," I offered, hoping for a useful response.

All I got back was a friendly, "Yes, be real careful."

By this time, I realized that my previous thoughts about a plan for surviving a fall from the bridge were stupid. If I was blown off, I was dead. The impact of hitting the water after such a long fall would surely knock me out, and it was stupid to think about surviving the freezing water. I had swum in Lake Michigan in August and knew how cold it was at this time of year. The correct plan was *not* to be blown off.

As I pulled away from the toll booth and worked my way through the gears, I felt that this was a strange bridge, different from others I had crossed. The guard rail seemed only knee-high. An optical illusion? I remained in the center.

It was too dark to see the Great Lakes below—Lake Michigan on my left and Lake Huron on my right. Shoals, heavy fog and high seas in the highly navigated waters between the two Great Lakes contributed to the loss of many ships in the area. Nine major wrecks lie within the Straits of Mackinaw in the 80-120 ft. depth range.

I concentrated on my riding and avoided looking over the side. I didn't want to create additional distractions while crossing the phantasm that this bridge had become. The center consisted of the same steel grating that is used on drawbridges. As experienced riders know, these gratings, like parallel railroad tracks, are hazardous to vehicles with only two wheels. They are especially dangerous when wet or icy. After realizing that the center lane was like this the entire way across, I decided to take my chances and move to the lane closest to the guard rail.

Some rain now, lots of wind, but at least no ice. I concentrated on being relaxed on the controls. I felt greatly relieved when I contacted the pavement on the northern shore. The few minutes it took to cross "Big Mac" seemed like an eternity.

I was a few hours behind Gary Eagan, whose experience in crossing the bridge had been much different from mine. He ascended the bridge as the sun was setting to his left, over Lake Michigan. The sky was filled with spectacular shades of red.

Half of the sun was visible as it sank slowly below the horizon. And at that instant, a full moon, appearing half the size of the sun, was rising to his right, shining brightly above Lake Huron.

After the rally, Gary documented his experience while crossing the bridge:

"It was like the sun and moon were perfectly balanced on a teeter-totter. It was surreal—so incredibly beautiful that I wanted to stop the bike and just watch it. But not on *that* bridge.

"I guess that event probably happens one or two times a year there, when the sun is far enough north and the moon is full. It's impossible to describe how wonderful that was. I yelled and shouted halfway to Manistique on Highway 2. It was just what I needed to rejuvenate me and ease the disappointment of the problems I believed had cost me a shot at winning the Iron Butt.

"What I needed to remember was that this was the ride of a lifetime and that winning or losing the event really couldn't screw that up."

Frozen, Famished, and Fatigued

For me, the next several hours were the coldest of the rally. I recalled a parking lot conversation that I had with Eddie Metz before the start of the rally. Eddie said that during his first Iron Butt in 1993, he once found himself discouraged and wondering why he had put himself into the position of being so cold, wet, hungry, fatigued, and far from home. I also recalled a dinner conversation with Mike Kneebone several years before, when he was our house guest.

"After a week into it, many riders reach the stage where all they want to do is have it all over with," Mike had said. "Some quit, others continue but begin forgoing bonus opportunities and head for the final checkpoints like horses returning to the barn." Fortunately, things never got so bad that I considered quitting. I spent several years anticipating the rally, expecting it to be every bit as challenging as it turned out to be.

I spent the next several hours riding along the northern shore of Lake Michigan, a ride I had wanted to do for years. After several hours, the sky cleared. I regretted that I didn't have the luxury of stopping to enjoy the moon and stars reflecting off the water.

It's amazing that riders will continue to ride for hours in great discomfort to avoid stopping. They'll tolerate an enlarged bladder to minimize nature breaks, put up with a growling stomach or parched throat to postpone a food stop, ride in wet clothing to avoid the interruption of donning a rainsuit, or permit a headache to develop as a result of incessant wind noise rather than stop to insert earplugs. At one time or another, I've been guilty of all of these quirks.

Mike included advice in his long-distance riding tips about "stopping to go farther." His advice was offered because the phenomenon described above is so prevalent, even among riders who should know better. Stopping at appropriate intervals for meal breaks and rest doesn't cost the endurance rider time. It actually makes it possible to spend more time in the saddle.

On this cold dark night in Michigan's Upper Peninsula, I found myself succumbing to another of these temptations. Although I had stopped hours earlier to don my long underwear and electric vest, I was still cold. My heated handlebar grips were fully on, but the tops of my hands that weren't in contact with the handlebars were cold. But I wanted to keep riding. It was hard to believe that just six days ago I was sweltering in the desert heat in Arizona, questioning the wisdom of continuing to wear the heavy Aerostich in such hot weather.

I was also tired and hungry. At about 4:00 a.m., I stopped in Saint Ignace for gas and prolonged my stay in the warm convenience store by eating prepackaged sandwiches, having a few cups of coffee, and chatting with the clerk. I used the opportunity to embed myself into all the additional clothing I could cram between the Gore-Tex skin of the Aerostich and my own. I put on another couple of T-shirts and a few more pairs of socks. I could barely force my feet back into the boots, with the extra socks in place. It was difficult to bend over to zip my boots and I could hardly turn my head. It was difficult to zip the Aerostich closed because I had difficulty bending my arms to pull the zipper all the way up my neck.

When my frozen toes stopped tingling, I headed for the door and made my way to the motorcycle. I felt conspicuous. I imagined the clerk giggling at my overstuffed waddle. I also was reminded of my previous business partner's uncharitable remarks about the rally. He referred to it as the "Iron Butt and Empty Head Rally."

It occurred to me that there is an interesting similarity between motorcycle touring and another of my passions, SCUBA diving. Both sports involve special equipment that sometimes causes the participant to feel clumsy and look comical. What looks sillier than a diver walking backward on a beach toward the sea with mask, fins, and SCUBA gear in place? I felt that foolish as I struggled to swing my leg over the seat of the motorcycle without getting my foot stuck on the duffel bag that was lashed to the passenger seat. This motion was more difficult than usual since I couldn't turn my helmeted head far enough to see through my fogged-over faceshield.

"It sure is fortunate that you don't have to move much to operate one of these things," I thought, as I struggled to get my overstuffed and heavily padded body situated comfortably on the motorcycle. I cracked the faceshield open to let the cold air clear the fog from inside its surface, pointed the bike west toward Manistique, and thought some more about warm beaches.

After I became hooked on motorcycling, I lost interest in SCUBA diving and underwater photography. I had been a diver for more than 25 years, and Barb and my three sons were certified divers. Until I discovered motorcycles, we spent nearly all of our family vacations in warm tropical waters.

I was cold, tired, alone, and in the middle of nowhere. Instead of using vacation time to freeze my ass off in sub-20-degree weather, I could be sitting at a blackjack table in the barefoot casino at the Flamingo Beach Hotel on Bonaire. Barb and I could be deciding which dive location to do in the morning. We might be consulting the Navy Dive Tables—over a glass of wine, of course—to be sure we wouldn't risk the "bends" by exceeding permitted combinations of depth and time.

With diving, the Navy Dive Tables are available to help us calculate whether we are endangering ourselves by staying at it too long. On a motorcycle, printed tables aren't available. Each rider is entirely on his own and is responsible for deciding when he's passed his personal limits. *Entirely on his own.* Endurance riders had better enjoy their own company, because they get a lot of it. On the leg between San Diego and Ft. Lauderdale, I saw Ardys Kellerman at Meteor Crater for a few minutes. She was the only rider I met on that leg. And between Florida and Maine, I saw Jesse Pereboom for less than five minutes in Rhode Island. On this final leg from Maine back to Salt Lake City, I would not see another contestant until I arrived at the finish line.

Multiple Maladies

I was dealing with cold and exhaustion. Martin Hildebrandt was experiencing difficulties of a new variety. His computer equipment had stopped working for the fourth time while he was making his way through Vermont. He wasn't finding it easy to navigate without his computer display and he became lost twice. He cursed himself for not taking time to highlight his route on the paper maps after entering it into the computer. He was also irritated for having buried his flashlight deep down in his fully packed duffel bag. And to make matters worse, he was stopped for speeding for his third time since the start of the rally. A Vermont State Trooper pulled the German motorcycle to the side of the road for traveling 75 mph in a 55 mph zone.

Martin found the ride through the small Vermont villages stressful. The encounter with the law only increased his level of anxiety. He finally surrendered to exhaustion and checked in to what he described as the "worst motel in the world." He placed his wet Gore-Tex boots and leather pants over the heating unit of the motel room and lay down for a three-hour nap.

When he rose at 5:00 a.m., the boots were still wet and his injured ankle was swollen. He couldn't force his ankle into his boot, even with the boot unzipped. He could hardly get his foot through his pants. He filled the bathtub with cold water, soaked his foot, and used the time to review the last leg's bonuses. This was the first time he gave the bonuses any consideration since he left Maine.

Sitting in the seedy motel room with his swollen foot soaking in the tub, he began to feel stupid and embarrassed. Not only had he already passed hundreds of points in easy bonuses without being aware of them, but he felt that his dumb stunt with the lobster lunch and superfluous computer repair were at the expense of valuable sleeping. He thought about how ideally positioned he would have been to capture the giant 2,485-point bonus for riding to Blaine, Washington.

Blaine would have been tough for any rider at this point. The most direct route to Salt Lake City via Blaine would have been across Canada, riding more than 3,800 miles in 72 hours. Averaging more than 53 mph for three days in a row after what the riders had already been through was all but impossible. The shortest route through the Unites States would have required riding more than 4,100 miles at an average speed of 57 mph.

When the swelling in his foot decreased enough to get the boot around it, Martin left for Hayward, Wisconsin. After reviewing the bonuses, he decided to stop for the photograph of the large fish at the Freshwater Fisherman Hall of Fame. He decided that he could capture this 816-point bonus and another 173 points for the Sherman Mountain Information Sign on I-80 on his way back to Salt Lake City. Like many of the riders, Martin was eager to bring the rally to an end. But for Martin, the end wouldn't come without one more encounter with American law enforcement authorities.

On his way to Eau Claire, Wisconsin, Martin was shivering with the cold, but was resisting stopping to add warmer clothing. Passing a slow-moving unmarked patrol car, Martin was given an excuse to stop. "An unfriendly, obese middle-aged officer looked at my German license plate and decided to give me a warning for doing 75 mph on the interstate," Martin related.

"This is as gracious as I can be," growled the officer. "And don't forget—this isn't the Autobahn."

For Martin, getting in and out of Hayward from Eau Claire looked easier than it turned out to be. It might have been easier if his computer had still been working. After he reached Hayward he missed an important junction and found himself lost in the wilderness.

"My computer was broken and the maps seemed to make little sense. Every road sign seemed to laugh at me. It seemed to take forever for me to find I-94 so that I could continue west to Fargo and the Dakotas."

Jesse in Jeopardy

At this point, the rally had all but destroyed Jesse Pereboom. Upon leaving Maine, Jesse had selected a route to Michigan through Canada. Once in Canada the weather turned cold. Jesse hadn't packed his severe cold weather gear. Like Gary Eagan, his Canadian journey included freezing rain, sleet, and snow. He waited shivering for more than an hour in line at the customs station, sitting on his motorcycle in the freezing rain waiting to cross back into the United States.

When he crossed back into Michigan he was tired, frozen, and hungry. He searched for a motel room in the cold rain from 2:00 a.m. until 5:00 a.m. He finally gave up outside Detroit, parked his bike under the awning of a strip mall, and slept on the sidewalk for an hour. He felt no better when he awakened. At 7:00 a.m. he found a motel room and crashed for three hours. He wanted more sleep, but knew that if he indulged himself he risked being time-barred in Salt Lake City.

Jesse recalled that many of his friends had laughed and predicted that he would never make it even halfway. He had invested a lot of time and money in this escapade and was determined to finish. But things got worse when he became ensnared in a Chicago traffic jam. He was so confused and fatigued that he didn't know what to do. He broke down and cried for ten minutes while sitting in the Chicago traffic.

Sylvan Settings

The roads getting in and out of Hayward were narrow and slow. The Fresh Water Fishing Hall of Fame was a great bonus, worth 816 points. It was easy to see why, considering the trouble to get to it. At least it was a beautiful, sunny day.

At 24 years old, Jesse Pereboom is the youngest rider to complete the Iron Butt.

Hayward was difficult to reach and the roads were agonizingly slow, but even in my exhausted state I marveled at the beauty of the Wisconsin wilderness. State Route 77 from Ironwood to Hayward was a thin, black "other principal road" according to Rand McNally. As the road weaved its way through the Chequamegon National Forest and skirted the Lac Courte Oreilles Indian Reservation, I passed one tranquil lakeside setting after another.

Clam Lake, Ghost Lake, Teal Lake, Lost Land Lake, Spider Lake, Round Lake, and finally Hayward, located on the banks of the Namekagon River. I mentally placed this area at the top of my list of new discoveries that demand a return when I don't have to ride more than 1,000 miles a day.

While I was reflecting on the tranquillity of the Wisconsin Forest, Marty Jones was enjoying the majesty of the Colorado Rockies while having an early lunch at the top of Pikes Peak near Colorado Springs. Marty was enjoying the same view that inspired Katherine Lee Bates, a Massachusetts author and teacher, to compose the lyrics to "America the Beautiful" 102 years earlier. Marty and Katherine surpassed Lt. Zebulon Montgomery Pike, who discovered the mountain in 1806. Pike's only attempt to climb the mountain was unsuccessful due to a cold November storm, and Pike later predicted that no one would ever reach the summit.

Marty picked up 452 points for climbing 14,110 feet and negotiating the 156 hair-raising turns on the world's second highest highway. He hoped that his climb above the clouds would make up for his negligence in failing to collect a toll receipt at the Kansas Turnpike earlier in the morning.

Sixty miles west of the point where he had exited the Kansas Turnpike, Marty had once again been stopped for speeding. The officer was friendly and didn't delay him long before sending him on his way. He then realized that he had neglected to collect a receipt worth 189 points when he exited the turnpike. Not believing that he had time to return and still collect the larger bonuses in Colorado, he continued west.

I finally found the Hall of Fame and took a picture of the giant fish statue at the front of the building, with my motorcycle and pink towel in the foreground. Then I headed for Shell Lake, Wisconsin. When I reached Shell Lake at noon, Jim Culp was 350 miles south of me, battling flu-like symptoms as he struggled to make his way back to Salt Lake City. For Jim, it was now a final push of less than 1,100 miles across I-80. He had "hit the wall" yesterday in Ohio. He hadn't had trouble staying awake; instead, he felt weak and shaky and seemed to be either too hot or too cold.

Jim tried to relieve the discomfort by forcing himself to drink a lot of liquids and to eat better. When he reached Des Moines, he decided just to head for the finish and disregard additional bonuses, except for the easy one at the Sherman Mountain sign on the interstate. He'd had to drop out of the 1993 rally due to electrical problems. This year he was determined to finish.

Energy Exhausted

I intended to collect more bonuses. During my last conversation with Barb earlier in the day, she warned me that it seemed to her that I was farther away than I realized. I wasn't listening. I had called to assure her that I was OK. I tried to avoid an urge to act cranky, but I wasn't receptive to advice. No one knew better than I did that I was capable of collecting bonuses in Montana, the Dakotas, and Colorado.

I rode through Fairbault, Minnesota, and Williams, Iowa. Until this point, I felt that I had been driving relatively safely and was proud of myself for keeping the adrenaline in check. I assumed it was resting inside me somewhere, in reserve and ready to spring to my rescue if necessary. I had been letting it rest since my cross-traffic exit in the rain in Jacksonville, Florida.

In a short time, three experiences caused me to acknowledge that I had to stop to sleep. First, while standing at the gas pump in Williams, I stumbled into the motorcycle and knocked one of the mirrors to the ground, nearly falling down in the process. While leaving the station, I took the left lane of a two-way frontage road, thinking it was one-way, and nearly headed into an oncoming car.

I vowed to tolerate only one more slip. Another transgression and I would pack it in for the night. Stopping would be difficult because I thought I was a contender but needed all available time on the motorcycle to collect more bonuses. Stopping now would cost me several places in the standings. I struggled to stay awake. I rode south on I-35 to Des Moines and headed west on I-80 without realizing that I was passing up an easy 196 points by neglecting to buy gasoline in Des Moines. I had overlooked the opportunity when I had examined the bonus sheets back in Maine. I wouldn't realize the mistake until after the rally.

I fought the "nods" more than at any time since the rally began. I tried every trick I knew. I opened the face shield to my helmet and stood upright on the pegs to let fresh air blast directly into my face, unobstructed by the motorcycle's windshield. I unzipped the front of the Aerostich to let air blow into the suit. I performed deep knee-bends while standing on the pegs, hoping that increasing my circulation would help me remain alert. I sat back down and shook my head vigorously from side to side. I changed my position on the motorcycle dramatically, trying to make myself as uncomfortable as possible. I ate a Snickers and drank a Mountain Dew. I sat on the passenger seat with my feet on the passenger pegs, my back pressed against the duffel bags, and my arms stretched forward on the controls. I sang, cursed, and shouted commands to myself to stay awake.

"Stay awake until sunrise, damn it! You can last until sunrise! Don't surrender now! Don't be such a damn wimp! After sunrise, things will be OK!"

I believed things would be OK if I could last until daylight. No matter how tired I get, I always become re-energized when I see sunshine. When I start a ride before daylight, I'm usually sluggish and drowsy, even after a good night's sleep. When the sun comes up, things improve.

Even before participating in endurance rallies I'd had plenty of experience with sleep deprivation and with the dramatic improvement in alacrity that accompanies the sun. Shortly after my assignment in Spain and a year before my relocation to Brazil, my company assigned me responsibility for building our management consulting business in Mexico, Central and South America, Japan, and Asia. To demonstrate their sense of humor, the company later added Canada and the Middle East to the list.

The world, minus the United States and Europe, was my territory. I traveled constantly and spent countless nights in airplane seats instead of beds. To avoid the need to continuously change my watch (and sometimes forget if I had done so) it remained set to Greenwich Mean Time. I once told a gathering of friends that I had tricked my circadian rhythms so frequently that it would take years to get them back into synch. I quipped that my body and I seldom have the chance to share the same time zone.

It seems that we have all been programmed to be sleepy in the wee hours of the morning and to be awake and alert when a new day begins. I wanted to milk the miracle just once more. I wanted to make it to daylight once again without stopping. I struggled and postponed my last allowable mistake for almost two hours. Finally, after running the motorcycle onto the shoulder of the road near Walnut, Iowa, I knew that I wouldn't see the next sunrise at all unless I stopped to sleep. Daylight was eight hours away. I just couldn't make the stretch.

I became choked up twice during the rally. First, when I passed under Brian Bush's video equipment suspended over the roadway leading from the motel parking lot in Salt Lake City. The second time was when I exited I-80 in Walnut, Iowa. I would have done anything to be able to continue riding; to not have to give in this close to the end. It had been 48 hours since I rose from my sleep in Maine and I couldn't last any longer.

There were no vacancies at the first motel where I stopped, so the clerk directed me to another. I briefly considered interpreting this as a sign that I should get back on the motorcycle and keep riding. Why not allow myself just one more mistake? After all, I had just demonstrated that I was capable of dismounting the motorcycle without dropping it, hadn't I? I made it to the check-in counter and back to the motorcycle without falling down. If I could do that, why couldn't I keep going?

As I pulled away from one motel in search of another, I tried to remind myself that my original goal was to finish my first Iron Butt while avoiding the catastrophic DNF curse. Considering my earlier difficulties in Florida and my loss of receipts in Texas, I should be pleased. I shouldn't push karma too far. The rally really wasn't to die for.

I checked into the next motel and put in a wake-up call for 4:00 a.m. This was the latest I could sleep while still having a chance to pick up Denver bonuses.

Bob Higdon's September 8th Internet correspondence, *Day Ten – Riding Home,* did a masterful job of capturing both the spirit and the essence of the closing hours of the rally:

> *In its final hours this edition of the Iron Butt Rally is reverting to form. In 1993 Steve Attwood walked away from the field, but his finish is not typical. Most rallies are lost, not won, in the closing hours by exotic mistakes that can be explained only by a psychiatrist. In the '91 IBR the difference between first and third place was six points. Ron Major was the beneficiary of crushing, unbelievable errors by two other*

riders mere hours from the rally's conclusion. It could be true in 1995.

One day Eddie James, who held a tiny 16-point lead over Marty Jones in Maine, will explain to his grandchildren why he decided to visit Reading, PA for 117 points. Of the 34 possible bonus sites on the Maine, to Utah leg, none—I repeat, none—is worth fewer points. He'll tell them how much time he lost riding through the awful, mountainous state roads instead of steaming west on an interstate highway at flank speed toward Colorado where the real bonus locations were. He may mention that he left his camera, and the Polaroid photo that was proof of his visit to the worthless bonus site, behind. He'll tell them, but they won't believe it.

. . . Marty Jones, nipping at Eddie James's heels, was believed to have captured the mother lode of bonuses near Denver by mid-Friday and may have headed to Yellowstone Park for more. If true, he is superbly positioned and could be the man to beat. He has run a flawless rally.

Doubts Develop Desperation

Eddie James, an experienced rider with a burning desire to win this rally, knew that the final point spread between top finishers is usually very thin. And Eddie, in first place upon leaving the final checkpoint of the rally, must have been experiencing both elation and anxiety—elation knowing that the sought-after goal was within his reach, anxiety because Marty, or another rider, could put in an outstanding performance during this crucial leg and deny him the victory he craved.

It's impossible for a rider to know which bonuses other riders have decided to pursue. With judgment becoming increasingly fallible with the fatigue of so many thousands of miles, it's difficult to predict what others are capable of accomplishing during the closing hours of the rally. At such times, it's easy to imagine the worst.

So it's likely that Eddie envisioned his potential victory slipping away beneath the rapidly spinning wheels of some unknown rider. His anxiety may have been heightened by his mistake of selecting a poor bonus choice and then losing the evidence of even that poor selection. His fellow riders wouldn't discover until days after the rally how he bent the rules to help secure a position among the top finishers. Knowing that he would be unable to make it to the American Heritage Motorcycle Museum in Westerville, Ohio, before it closed, Eddie enlisted the help of a friend who worked at the museum. His friend agreed to meet him at the museum to furnish a business card to prove that the visit had been made.

Bob's entry for the day ended with the following sentiment:

> *When the sun drops over the yardarm tomorrow afternoon, it will begin to sear the riders' eyes as they plow west. Mentally, they will calculate the hours remaining, the miles yet to go, and their chances of sliding into the narrow time window that opens at 1700 MDT. They will return to the motel parking lot that they left 264 hours and so many, many miles ago.*
>
> *They know the way home. They just have to get there. Somehow.*

Competitors Converge on Closure

Dozens of riders were strung out along I-80 for hundreds of miles. They were strung out both figuratively and literally— mostly, literally. If my imaginary tracking system were a reality, the giant screen would now show slightly more than 30 squiggly lines converging on Salt Lake City, mostly along this one interstate highway.

September 1995						
Mon	Tue	Wed	Thur	Fri	Sat	Sun
28	29	30	31	1	2	3
4	5	6	7	8	9	10
11	12	13	14	15	16	17
18	19	20	21	22	23	24
25	26	27	28	29	30	

As I was sleeping in a motel beside I-80, murf was checking in to a motel in Rawlins, Wyoming, less than 300 miles from Salt Lake City and almost 700 miles closer to the finish than I. Murf reported making good time through Iowa and Nebraska until he took the U.S. Highway 26 cutoff to Scottsbluff, Nebraska. "About 15 miles into the bonus project the skies turned black and the rain came down," he said. "I chickened out and went back to I-80 in order to make sure that I arrived at my target of Rawlins, Wyoming. Picking up the Sherman Mountain bonus was nothing compared to the loss of my low beam, horizontal rain, rough grooved pavement, and the downhill run to Laramie."

Karol Patzer was on the same highway, but in Sidney, Nebraska, about halfway between murf and me. She pulled into a gasoline station at 2:30 a.m. Like murf, who passed through Sidney hours before, Karol considered making a side trip to Scottsbluff that would have added about 90 miles to her trip. She decided the additional hour and a half on secondary roads wasn't worth the 201 points the trip would add to her score. Besides, she reminded herself, it was a lot more important to finish than to collect additional bonuses. She just wanted to be finished.

Unbeknownst to Karol, Jim Culp, who had helped her get her bike upright at her first bonus stop of the rally, was also in Sidney, asleep in a nearby motel. Jim had given up the quest for more bonuses and decided to get a decent night's rest on the last evening of the rally.

After Karol had a cup of coffee, she noticed another rider at another set of gasoline pumps. The rider looked strange—in the cold, he was wearing coveralls and had a sweatshirt tied around his head. As she approached she recognized Rick Morrison. Rick's helmet was stolen when he left it sitting on his motorcycle at a gas stop in Pennsylvania. The only helmet he could find, at a Harley-Davidson dealer, was too large. Wearing the sweatshirt around his head helped the size problem and helped with the cold as well.

"Rick followed me around, chattering constantly," Karol reported. "He finally suggested that I should just leave, since he hadn't seen anyone for days and didn't want to shut up."

Karol had come upon Rick days before, asleep in the grass at a rest area on the way to Maine. Rick missed the Maine checkpoint, partly because he overslept. He spent a full six hours asleep in the grass—four hours longer than he had intended. When I heard this story later, I wished I had been there to wake him and return the favor from my first night at the Iron Butt Motel in Utah.

Jesse Pereboom, several hundred miles behind Karol, realized he had been riding in a daze and pulled in to a rest area at 3:00 a.m. to find the husband and wife McAteers there, trying to muster enough strength to avoid the damned DNF disaster. Jesse couldn't understand why they hadn't killed each other by now, as they were riding two-up on a motorcycle that Jesse considered much less comfortable than his own. The McAteers were in tears. They wanted to finish so badly, but didn't know how they could. His conversation with them gave Jesse the boost that he needed to push on.

By the time Karol reached Cheyenne, she had been riding almost continuously for 26 hours and had covered 1,400 miles. She tried to get a room, and was sent from one fully occupied motel to another. She finally found one with a vacancy at 4:00 a.m. but had to wake the manager.

When Karol asked for the room, the manager wanted to know where her partner was. When she said she was alone, the manager shook his head and grunted, "Crazy country, women running around alone at night."

Anxiety Attack

Karol's check-in corresponded almost precisely with my checkout. When my wake-up call came at 4:00 a.m., I hit the road again. With the benefit of some sleep and a new look at the atlas, I realized I was in big trouble. Barb was right. The challenge before me was to make it to Salt Lake as close to 5:00 p.m. as possible to preserve as many points as I could. Forget additional bonuses!

I was nearly 1,000 miles from the finish and had about 13 hours before the checkpoint was scheduled to open, 15 hours before I would be time-barred. Although I didn't calculate it at the time, I had to *average* about 77 mph, including fuel stops, to arrive in time to keep all my bonus points. I would have to make a full day's distance, even by Iron Butt standards, in little more than *half* a day. Not a trivial accomplishment after ten consecutive 1,000-mile days.

Karol Patzer had the stock fuel tank of her K75S modified to extend her range. *Photo by Steve Johnson.*

There were several occasions during the rally when I promised myself that the next time I felt worried, stressed out, or overworked, I would chastise myself for whining and would be thankful that at least I didn't have to ride a motorcycle another 1,000 miles. This was one of those occasions.

Contemplating Completion

Meanwhile, Gary Eagan was searching for the entrance to the Theodore Roosevelt National Park, a bonus location in the western part of North Dakota. The bonus was worth another 263 points—if he could find it. At this point Gary had "hit the wall" and wasn't able to ride for more than half an hour or so without stopping for a 10- or 15-minute nap. So when he couldn't find the bonus, he did the same thing that he had done when he failed to find the Biltmore Mansion in North Carolina: he said "the hell with it" and pushed on, after having ridden to within a few miles of the bonus. Gary had collected a giant 468-point bonus in Minot, North Dakota, 225 miles east of his current position. Then he collected a speeding ticket from a North Dakota State Trooper—for doing 68 mph in a 55 mph zone. It was Gary's second traffic citation of the rally.

Jan Cutler introduced the term "power nap" into the vocabulary of endurance riding to describe the way Gary kept himself going. He pulled to the side of the road, in a rest area if possible, placed his gloves on the pavement to provide slight elevation for his helmeted head, and slept on the concrete.

The Marine Corps teaches foot soldiers that when their body can go no further, they can get only the bare minimum of sleep they need to go and still wake up—as long as they don't get too comfortable. If they undress and cover up, they'll be out for hours. Stay on the motorcycle, rest your head on the tank bag, or adopt the Eagan technique, and in less than a half-hour's time, you'll awaken refreshed enough to continue for a period of time. Although the usefulness of this technique has limits, many endurance riders use a version of it when they are exhausted but must ride a while longer.

As Gary was benefiting from one of these power naps on the final leg of the rally, he was shaken awake by two concerned motorists. I'm certain he wasn't intentionally rude, although he insists he wasn't capable of speaking anything resembling English at the time.

As dawn was breaking, Martin Hildebrandt was waking from his last two hour nap of the rally. He had pulled behind a gasoline station in North Platte, Nebraska, to rest. Martin described the scene a short while later when he stopped for gasoline:

"Heading down the road I turned into a fuel station and felt as though I was coming home when I saw Suzy Johnson and Chuck Pickett at the pumps.

"Chuck walked to me. Neither of us spoke a word as we embraced and exchanged hugs that were more than only sincere. We felt the same honest happiness that two brothers feel after a separation of 20 years. Bystanders appeared puzzled. I'm 6′2″ and Chuck is as large. We both had full and filthy beards and were in dirty and stinking motorcycle clothes. Neither of us was bothered by that. In one sense, I and this man didn't know much about each other. I've never seen his home and he hasn't seen mine. We hadn't spoken more than a few dozen words to each other before we left Salt Lake City. But now, 11 days later, we know that we share an experience that can't be bought at any shop. We've seen the same ghosts in the same nights. We both fought them and beat them. This isn't something many people can tell about each other."

This poignant scene captures the feeling that many riders were experiencing during the final days of the rally.

Suzy and Chuck decided to have a full breakfast and stayed as Martin continued on. Martin wanted to reserve an additional time cushion in case something should happen. As he drove down I-80, totally exhausted with concentration fading, he just wanted to end the pain and tiredness. He drove slowly, not wanting to have an accident and not wanting to be stopped again for speeding. He just wanted to be done.

Big Bonus Bypass

Considering the early morning hour and the open country, I was able to go like a bat out of hell for three tanksfull of gasoline, through Waco and Lexington, Nebraska. I continued to Big Springs, Nebraska, and through Cheyenne, Rawlins, and Green River, Wyoming.

The last bonus a rider could capture was on the median strip of the interstate highway between Cheyenne and Laramie. I stopped the motorcycle and snapped a photo of the Sherman Mountains information sign. Although this was the easiest bonus of the rally, worth a hefty 173 points, many riders failed to collect it. Riders who had ridden hundreds of miles for 50 points on the first day of the rally wouldn't even take a few moments to collect the easy 173 points sitting alongside the highway. Some didn't pay attention as they passed the parking area. Others didn't want to take the time to stop.

Jerry Clemmons admits that his last day on the road was the most totally focused of his riding career. He knew he was passing this last bonus, but had no intention of stopping. Jerry just wanted to get back to Salt Lake City. Horst Haak and Hank Rowland had also agreed that they wouldn't bother stopping again until they hit Salt Lake City. After the rally I asked Hank if he had collected the Sherman Mountain information sign bonus.

"I cannot tell a lie," Hank confessed. "As I passed the bonus, I saw several bikes off to the left. When my brain finally connected and I realized that I had just passed the bonus, I was already down the road—so toasted that I didn't want to go back. I didn't even know if Horst was still riding with me or not by that point. And I didn't really care."

Karol Patzer admitted that she would have sped by without stopping if she hadn't seen the bikes of other riders who had parked to capture the shot. Karol returned to collect the bonus, but saw other contestants speed by with no attempt to stop.

Charles Elberfeld stopped and took a picture of an information sign, but forgot to record his odometer reading at the bonus location, part of the required ritual for the collection of bonuses. Later, when he attempted to calculate what the odometer would have indicated by calculating the difference between mile markers, he realized that he had taken a picture of the wrong sign. Although he had time to return to do the bonus correctly, he tossed the worthless photo in the trash and tried to keep his feeling of embarrassment in check as he negotiated the ribbon of slab wending its way to Utah.

Martin Hildebrandt stopped to photograph the sign and was amused to see that a rider had left his towel hanging on the sign after the photograph was taken. Martin didn't know if this was an oversight or intentional. At least the rider wouldn't need the towel again.

After photographing his Helix at the information sign, Ed Otto became totally focused on getting to Salt Lake City in time to avoid being time-barred. He had leg cramps. His butt hurt so badly that it hurt to try to shift into a more comfortable position. He was hungry and thirsty, but felt that he couldn't afford to stop for food. The thought of Steve Chalmers with his time clock in hand motivated him to push on to the finish line.

Things were tough everywhere. Riders coming in from the southeast passed up plenty of easy points too. Boyd Young, fighting to pull himself back into the top ten after his poor fourth leg, managed to collect the 281-point bonus at the Pro Rodeo Hall of Fame in Colorado Springs, then fell asleep for an hour while sitting on his motorcycle in the parking lot. The bonus was relatively easy to collect, if you were coming up I-25, as the site was 100 yards from the highway. Boyd intended to collect 181 more points by visiting Gunnison on his way to the finish, but decided instead to ignore it, even though the trip to Gunnison would have added only 20 miles and half an hour to his ride. Boyd knew it, but he just didn't care. He was too tired to even *think* about another bonus. Besides, his motorcycle wasn't at its peak. He wouldn't learn until he returned to Oklahoma that his motorcycle had a broken exhaust valve.

We were like horses heading for the barn at the end of a long day, just as Mike Kneebone had told me at our dinner table four years earlier.

Riders Return

While I was still several hours from the finish, Jerry Clemmons was already pulling into the motel parking lot in Salt Lake City, the first rider to cross the finish line. Jerry arrived so early that Brian Bush's video crew was caught by surprise and had to ask Jerry to re-enact his arrival for the camera.

Rick Morrison also arrived in Salt Lake City hours before the final checkpoint opened. Unlike Jerry, Rick couldn't bring himself to ride directly to the finish line. First, he felt the need to "get things right with myself."

After oversleeping beside the road in Virginia and missing the Maine checkpoint, Rick was very angry with himself. Missing the checkpoint not only resulted in heavy penalties but also barred him from collecting bonuses on this final leg. His anger and frustration grew during the final hours of the rally as he anticipated acknowledging his blunder to his fellow riders.

When he reached Salt Lake City, Rick rode downtown to a park, lay on the grass, and stared at the clouds. It would have been easier to accept a DNF caused by mechanical failure or an accident. It was a lot more difficult to accept a poor finishing position because of his own mistakes. Rick had his own collection of "if onlies" to deal with. After taking a few hours to reflect

Jerry Clemmons, dressed in Iron Butt hat and jacket—presents from his in-laws. Jerry claims they were getting tired of seeing him dressed in his Iron Butt T-shirts.

on the events of the last 11 days, he was ready to enter the parking lot of the Airport Quality Inn to conclude his role in this extraordinary event.

The excerpt from Bob Higdon's dispatch for the last day of the rally described the scene at the motel parking lot as the riders returned. Bob dubbed this final report *Day Eleven – On the Flight Deck, the Fat Lady Warms Up:*

> *It was a scene from a grade B movie. The grizzled admiral, Steve Chalmers, stood on the bridge of the aircraft carrier, which looked remarkably like a motel parking lot in Salt Lake City, wondering where his pilots were. Beside him was his adjutant, Mike Kneebone, trying unsuccessfully to hide his anxiety. He knew that some of the planes would not be returning from this mission.*
>
> *Gastonia, North Carolina Gold Wing pilot Jerry Clemmons was the first to touch down on the deck. He slowly unbolted*

himself from the bike, smiled wanly, and said, "I ride a lot. Back home everyone knows me for doing big miles. But these guys whipped my butt." He took his evidence towel out, the shocking pink one with his rider number stenciled prominently on it. For 11 days he had hung the towel on signs and photographed it as proof of his having visited a bonus site. Now he simply wiped his face with it. For pilot Clemmons the ordeal was over . . .

At 12:30 the first of the true aces, Tom Loegering, popped out of the sky on his fearsome BMW dual-sport R1100GS, a dirt bike with an attitude. In heroic fashion he had just crushed another leg and instantly became the man to beat . . .

One who could do just that, customs agent Marty Jones, showed up next. He too had grabbed a fistful of bonuses on the final leg. Would it be enough? . . .

In the final minutes before the checkpoint opened and the lateness penalties began to accumulate, Jesse Pereboom on his Harley battlewagon dove into view. "They said it would burn up in the desert," he smiled. "It didn't."

Tired, Tardy, and Testy

All this fun in the parking lot, and I was still attempting to get to Salt Lake City without being time-barred. While approaching Green River, I passed a Honda Shadow and exchanged waves with the rider. I took the next exit for gas. By the time I finished refueling, the Shadow pulled up and the rider got off, examining my motorcycle while I paid for my purchase.

When I returned, the rider wanted to engage me in conversation, and although I was late, he seemed like a nice fellow and I didn't want to be impolite. He noticed my Iron Butt license frame and expressed first interest, then incredulity, when he realized what I was doing.

"Hell, I like riding too, but after 350 miles I want to be home to sit down with a drink and relax."

He mumbled to himself, at least three or four times, "11,000 miles in 11 days"? Then, "How old are you anyway?" Turns out he's at least ten years older. Finally I said, "I really have to get going," but still felt a bit guilty for being rude to a fellow enthusiast.

It was 3:15 p.m. and I knew I would be late to Salt Lake. The final two-hour window would open at 5:00 p.m. I would have to *average* almost 100 mph for the last 165 miles to arrive when the checkpoint opened. That wasn't going to happen. Making the two-hour window would require an average speed of only 45 mph, but I would lose ten points for each minute I was late.

I knew Barb was there and might begin to worry, but I couldn't take the time to call. Later I learned she was less worried than others who were awaiting my arrival. She had become part of this. She had been drawn into the excitement as if she too were a participant rather than an observer. She was concerned about the points I was losing with every passing minute.

I entered the parking lot of the motel at 6:17 p.m., 77 minutes into the window and running a nearly empty tank. Only a few people were milling around, since I was the last rider unaccounted for. As I stopped the bike and turned off the engine, Barb approached to take my picture. She had already shot half a roll of film of other riders as they entered the lot. She couldn't tell they weren't me until they removed their helmets.

I was still removing my equipment while Barb explained the concern that Steve Chalmers and other riders and checkpoint workers had expressed about my tardiness. Riders were instructed to notify rally officials as soon as they knew they were going to miss the checkpoint, and Mike Kneebone was anxiously awaiting either my arrival or my call. Except for riders who had already called with news to say they would miss this final checkpoint, I was the only rider "missing in action." Concerned that I may have left a message on the answering machine at Steve's home, Mike headed there shortly before my arrival at the motel. As people began putting their arms around her shoulders and reassuring her that everything would be okay, Barb began to worry that she *should* be worrying.

Earlier, Barb had told Mike of our last discussion before she left Plano for the airport to come to Salt Lake City, including my plan to attempt additional bonuses during the final day. "He's crazy!" Mike had told her. "There's no way he has time to make those bonuses, based on where he was when he called you."

The parking lot party was over, and riders who had already finished were bathing and resting in preparation for the celebration banquet that was to begin in less than an hour. I didn't see anyone from Brian's video crew. I was eager to shower, but had no time for a nap.

Steve approached with his hand extended to congratulate me for finishing. He invited me to his suite to complete the final check-in and debriefing. Although I was happy to be a qualified finisher, I was dejected about the loss of points associated with my late arrival, and with my inability to collect additional bonuses on this last leg.

As I submitted my last batch of receipts and bonus photos, Steve keyed the information into his laptop computer. He read the disappointment on my face.

Ten points per minute times 77 minutes—almost another thousand points down the drain. This late penalty alone completely erased the 701 points I had earned for crossing the bridge at Mackinaw City. The Iron Butt is not forgiving to riders whose reach exceeds their grasp.

"Just a few more questions," said Steve. "Did you get any traffic tickets?"

"No."

"Do you know of any violation of the rules by other riders that I should know about?"

"No."

Steve looked up from his PC and smiled. "You'll be pleased," he declared. He wouldn't tell me how I or the other riders finished. He was saving that for the banquet in a few minutes.

"I think I'll take a shower and change clothes," I said.

"Thanks," Steve replied. "Your fellow riders will appreciate that."

8

Awards Ceremony

The Survivors

A Fitting Finish

The banquet and festivities were a fitting conclusion to the rally. Brian Bush and his video crew were present to record the event for posterity.

When murf's Dom Perignon from Ft. Lauderdale was delivered to the tables, the tuxedoed murf delivered a toast in honor of the finishers. It was fortunate that he decided to place the call from Ft. Lauderdale, rather than wait until he returned to Salt Lake City. Being in Mormon country, the motel wasn't equipped to serve champagne and had to rent glasses.

The champagne was a great touch, as was murf's tuxedo. Treating the entire field of finishers to champagne was the kind of thing I would have liked to have thought of myself, but I would have been concerned about appearing foolish or ostentatious. Murf pulled it off beautifully.

Final standings were announced at the banquet and trophies distributed.

TOP STANDINGS

Standing	Rider	Miles Ridden	Points
1	Tom Loegering	11,881	20,727
2	Eddie James	11,679	20,195
3	Gary Eagan	12,266	19,992
4	Marty Jones	11,609	19,875
5	Martin Hildebrandt	9,736	17,982
6	Ron Major	11,227	17,369
7	Eugene McKinney	10,756	17,303
8	Ron Ayres	12,007	17,186
9	Michael Stockton	10,613	17,150
10	Morris Kruemcke	11,463	16,933

I had placed eighth overall, and was second for distance traveled, behind Gary Eagan. This in spite of my loss of bonuses and my late arrivals in Spokane, Ft. Lauderdale and Salt Lake City. My performance also qualified me, along with Gary Eagan, for one of endurance riding's most coveted awards, the "10/10ths Challenge," awarded to riders who have documented ten consecutive 1,000 mile-days.

Steve Chalmers announced that Garve Nelson had called to report that he intended to finish the rally, but wouldn't make it back to Salt Lake City in time for the banquet. He had simply run out of steam.

Hard to be Humble
Riders finishing first through fifth received trophies. Those collecting more than 17,500 points would earn a gold medal in addition to any other trophies or awards. Those collecting at least 13,751 points would earn a silver medal, and riders earning at least 10,250 points would earn bronze.

After dinner, Chalmers stood before the group to award the trophies: Plexiglas maps of the United States, engraved with the logo of the Iron Butt Association. The trophies varied in size, with the largest awarded to the first place finisher, along with the shirt that had been signed by the entrants over a week ago.

As Chalmers prepared to award the first place trophy to Tom Loegering, he referred to Tom's admirable performance in 1993, despite so many difficulties with his motorcycle that year.

Once Mike "murf" Murphy was confident he would finish, he arranged for champagne and his tuxedo to be shipped to the finishing line. Here, he strikes a dashing pose before the rider banquet.

188   Against the Wind

This year, Tom's performance included hitting all 48 contiguous states. Only he and Martin Hildebrandt had accomplished that.

Eddie James was clearly pleased with his second place trophy. He had managed to fulfill his "destiny" of placing among the top five finishers.

Gary Eagan, after accepting his third place trophy, entertained the group with his account of how he struggled to apply eye drops without first removing his sunglasses in New Mexico.

Marty Jones's fourth place finish was a vast improvement over his 1993 appearance, in which he was unable to finish due to injuries and a demolished motorcycle.

Martin Hildebrandt, who finished in fifth place, rode the most productive miles of the rally. He had covered fewer miles than any of the other top 14 finishers, but his 48-state bonus placed him above most of the field. Had he missed one state, say Providence, he would have finished in the middle of the pack.

I learned that Ron Major, equipped with his auxiliary fuel tank, stopped only 36 times during the rally to refuel. I stopped 84 times and nearly ran out of fuel on three occasions. Assuming an average of ten minutes for each stop, including completion of gas log and time required to enter and exit the service station, I spent eight hours more than Ron Major on non-productive refueling. I promised myself an auxiliary tank before my next endurance rally.

Ed Otto may have been riding a lawnmower-powered entry, but he bagged a silver medal and finished ahead of 15 more powerful machines, including Honda Gold Wings, ST1100s, BMWs, Harleys, a Yamaha Venture, an FJ1200, and a GSX-R1100.

Several riders remarked that they were captivated by the beauty of the country. Hank Rowland told the group that he was so impressed with what he had seen, he wished he was a poet so he could adequately describe his feelings about it. Despite the limited time that we had for sightseeing, I knew from remarks like Hank's that many of my comrades shared my appreciation for the reflective moments we enjoy while indulging our passion.

Rick Morrison, who has always named his motorcycles, reported that "Starbuck" had performed flawlessly, even though he felt like he was beating it to death at times. He was looking forward to giving it fresh oil and a good rest.

Jim Culp told the group how the same song, "Magic Carpet Ride" by Steppenwolf, kept running through his head during the entire rally. "After the first few hundred times, it almost got to be a mantra," Jim said.

After dropping out of his third Iron Butt in Florida, Rick Shrader had returned to Salt Lake City a day before the event ended. "Oh well, I guess I'll keep trying," he remarked with a note of sadness. I know I wasn't the only rider in the room who shared his disappointment. I also wasn't alone in feeling admiration and respect for his determination.

Gregg Smith, having just completed his fourth Iron Butt Rally, reported that this might have been his last. As Lorraine, his wife of 26 years, beamed at the prospect of his retirement, Gregg suggested that he plans to devise a relatively tame "Old Timers" version of the rally in which bonus points are awarded based on time spent in motels and restaurants.

David Kerslake, the only finisher riding a bona fide sport bike, discouraged others from attempting to do so. "Crotch rockets" just aren't intended to provide the degree of comfort available with a touring bike, he testified.

Chuck Pickett's comments evoked a lot of laughter, and several nods of understanding, when he thanked his ex-wives for divorcing him, thus making it possible for him to participate in an event like this.

Eddie Metz's comment was short and sweet: "My ass is sore."

Cheers for Chalmers
At the conclusion of the rider remarks, Chalmers received a standing ovation for having directed what many veterans described as the most well-run Iron Butt ever conducted.

Finally, we gathered for a group photograph. Top finishers took positions of honor in the front row, trophies proudly displayed on the floor before them. In addition to his trophy, Tom Loegering draped the Iron Butt T-shirt with 55 signatures across his knee. Lights flashed repeatedly as friends and family recorded this photo opportunity.

At the conclusion of the dining room festivities, Barb and I joined other riders in the lounge for cocktails and conversation. When I returned to my room I removed and disposed of my contact lenses for the first time since the rally began. I hadn't even opened my bottle of wetting solution.

Sunday, September 10

I slept later than usual Sunday morning. Later, Barb and I joined Suzy Johnson and Chuck Pickett in the motel restaurant to swap stories about the recently completed event. After breakfast, I met Tom Loegering in the corridor of the motel and congratulated him for his outstanding performance. Tom smiled shyly and replied, "Thanks, I guess I just got lucky."

I left Barb on her own to catch the motel shuttle back to the airport for her flight home, while I once again mounted the motorcycle for the trip back to Plano. As I was leaving I stopped to say good-bye to Leonard Aron, who was driving a small U-Haul truck. His Indian Chief was safely in the back for the ride home to Southern California. Leonard had covered 5,300 miles with the motorcycle before burning a hole in a piston in Georgia.

As I left Salt Lake City, I remembered how amazed I was to learn that most riders head home *by motorcycle* after the rally. Some ride well over a thousand miles to return home. I recall thinking that, after such a rally, riders surely would have had enough riding and wouldn't be looking forward to riding again.

Yet I loved being back on the motorcycle so soon. I welcomed the opportunity to ride at a relatively relaxed pace without having to worry about checkpoints or bonus stops. I knew that at some point during the trip home, probably in the middle of the night in the middle of the mountains, I would be struck with the brilliance and magnificence of the stars. I would be able to pull the motorcycle to the side of the road to spend a few minutes gazing at the heavens. I looked forward to that even more than the hot shower and cold beer that would accompany my end-of-the-day meal.

The obligatory group photo after the banquet.

As I was traveling home on I-70 in eastern Utah, I passed a large yellow traffic sign. I thought it read, "Eagles on Highway." I drove on for several minutes, wondering if my eyes could have deceived me. I had never before seen such a sign. Could I still be suffering the effects of sleep deprivation?

The American Bald Eagle is the corporate symbol adopted when my company was founded. The company's recruiting motto is "Eagles don't flock. You have to find them one at a time." Employees often refer to one another as "Eagles." Photography and art featuring this American symbol are prevalent throughout the corridors and offices of the company. One of the company's officers kept in his office a photograph of half a dozen or so eagles, flocked in a single tree, as if to mock the company's corporate slogan. Apparently, these eagles hadn't received our "anti-flocking" directive.

I had obtained my "real" camera and tripod from Barb as I departed Salt Lake City. I executed two consecutive U-turns, determined that the sign was not a fantasy, placed the motorcycle near the sign on the shoulder of the road, erected the tripod and camera, set the self-timer, and photographed myself leaning against the sign. Except for the photograph that Barb snapped upon my arrival back in Salt Lake City after the rally, this is my favorite memento of the trip.

Shortly before stopping at Poncha Springs, Colorado, for my last evening of the trip, I found a good spot to pull to the side of the road for some star-gazing. I recalled Hank Rowland's after-dinner comments to the group about wishing he was a poet so that he could describe how he felt. I knew exactly what he meant.

I caught this unusual sign on the highway near
Thompson, Utah, on my way home from the rally.
The eagle is the corporate symbol for my company.

Monday, September 11

The next morning, I stopped for a break at a rest stop south of Walsenberg, Colorado. I talked with two riders who were touring on Gold Wings. One of them noticed my Iron Butt license frame and asked if I had ever participated in the event. They were impressed to hear that I had just completed the rally and were eager to discuss it with me. This was my first experience with the prestige assigned to participants in the Iron Butt Rally.

Marty Jones, too, had a brush with fame. He was buying gas in New Mexico on his way back to Texas when a young man approached to ask if he could have his picture taken with Marty. The guy explained that he was an "Iron Butt fan" and wanted a picture of Marty holding his fourth place trophy.

When I entered Texas I began to think again about business and of the career decision that I had expected to ponder during the last two weeks. I had spent this entire period of time hardly thinking of work at all. On the few occasions when it crossed my mind, I quickly dismissed the thoughts and focused instead on the rally, my riding and daydreaming.

I pulled into a service station, walked to a public phone and called the company. I wanted to discuss my fate before the offices closed. It was just as well that I hadn't spent a lot of time contemplating options. In my absence, the company decided to encourage me to accept a Plano-based position with one of the company's largest business units.

When I arrived home shortly before midnight, my odometer showed I had covered 14,530 miles since leaving home two weeks before.

Tuesday, September 12

The staff at BMW of North Dallas in Plano knew I had entered the Iron Butt. They had no idea how I was going to finish. When I told Carl, the owner of the shop, of my finishing position he was suitably impressed.

I looked for George Mitmanski to report the results of the rally and to honor the promise I'd made to myself while sitting in the pouring rain alongside my revived motorcycle in Jacksonville nearly a week before. After I expressed my appreciation, he disabled my sidestand cutoff switch.

George Mitmanski not only opened the BMW dealership in Plano, Texas, on a Sunday morning to service the author's motorcycle, he also provided some much needed advice during the rally.

9

Winners' Losses

Disqualifications

Shortly after the rally, I received a letter from Steve Chalmers stating that Eddie James, the second place finisher, had been disqualified for a violation of the rules and that all riders moved up one place in the standings.

At some point after leaving Gorham, Eddie called a friend for help in collecting 354 bonus points. He rode to the American Heritage Motorcycle Museum in Westerville, Ohio. The mileage that he had recorded from his odometer properly reflected that he made the ride, but he arrived after the museum closed. His friend provided him with a business card to prove that he made the visit. Although the visit had been made, the bonus was valid only if collected during the hours that the museum was open to the public, and to other riders.

When confronted with the violation, Eddie admitted the deed and volunteered to forfeit the ill-gotten bonus points. He insisted that when he handed in the receipts he told both Mike Kneebone and Steve Chalmers, as well as other riders, about the circumstances surrounding the acquisition of the receipts. Mike and Steve didn't recall the conversation.

Steve believed that sacrificing points wasn't enough. That would suggest that violations are okay if not detected. He disqualified Eddie and asked that the trophy be returned. Although Eddie was disappointed, he returned his trophy with a minimum of fuss.

Several days later, I received another letter from Steve stating that the winner, Tom Loegering, was also disqualified for an infraction of the rules. Garve Nelson was disqualified for participating in the violation.

Somewhere in Arkansas, Tom had lost his towel. Without his towel, he would be unable to collect bonuses requiring photographs for the duration of the rally. Unlike Gary Eagan, Eddie Metz, and probably a few other riders as well, Tom didn't backtrack to retrieve the towel. Instead, he decided to abandon a "top ten" goal, go for the 48 states, take it easy, and enjoy himself. When he reached Florida, he pulled into a filling station to refuel and met Garve Nelson, whose goal was simply to complete the rally by going from one checkpoint to another. He didn't care about bonus points. When Tom told Garve about his lost towel, Garve offered Tom his own towel. Because each rider had a unique number assigned to him, Garve altered the towel by attaching makeshift numbers fashioned with electrical tape to the back side of the towel. The back of the towel now had Tom's number rather than Garve's.

"We'll have fun telling the other riders about this after the rally," said Garve, as Tom headed off to collect more bonus points.

Tom didn't give in to Steve Chalmers's decision as easily as Eddie had. He sent a letter to Steve, with copies to all participating riders, contesting the disqualification on the grounds that he had actually ridden all of the miles himself, had visited all bonus locations in which the fraudulent towel had been used, and was being disqualified on the basis of unclear verbal rules.

At the checkpoint in Ft. Lauderdale, Tom had asked Mike Kneebone if the primary purpose of the towel was to provide proof that the rider had visited the bonus locations. Mike confirmed that this was indeed the purpose of the towel. Tom

At 72 years old, Garve Nelson was the oldest, back to defend his title of the oldest rider to complete the rally. Except for Ed Otto's Honda Helix, Garve's Honda Ascot was the smallest motorcycle of the field.

interpreted the statement to mean that it was permissible for him to use Garve's towel.

Because Tom mailed his objection letter to the riders, Steve Chalmers addressed a copy of his reply to the riders as well. Steve dismissed Tom's request for reinstatement on the basis that he had clearly violated the rules of the rally. Steve insisted that the rules applied equally to all riders and requested that Tom return the signed T-shirt to the "now rightful" first place finisher, Gary Eagan.

I believe most riders backed Steve's decision. Garve's disqualification was disappointing because of his popularity and apparent desire to be helpful to another rider. His actions weren't intended to improve his own standing in any way. Because Garve didn't make it back to Salt Lake City for the awards ceremony and banquet, we can only speculate as to whether the story of the substitute towel would have unfolded as Tom implied.

I knew that Steve was receiving flak from some quarters, particularly for disqualifying Garve. I sent him an e-mail message supporting what I thought must have been a difficult decision for him. It would have been easier for him to limit the disqualifications to Eddie and Tom. Riders would not have demanded Garve's disqualification. Steve disqualified Garve because he felt it was the right thing to do.

At Mike Kneebone's urging, Tom finally returned the shirt. The controversy surrounding the disqualifications continued. Several riders considered the disqualifications too harsh. They contended that Iron Butt history includes incidents in which riders tried to bend the rules, were caught and embarrassed, but were permitted to continue the rally. In the most well-known episode, a rider tried to secure a poker chip from a Las Vegas casino. The violating rider tried to avoid a long ride by sitting at an immigration station on the California border and offering to buy a chip from any incoming motorist who had retained one. Although he was able to obtain the chip, he was denied credit for the bonus points when Mike caught him.

A few critics based their argument on the spirit of previous Iron Butt competitions, especially the previous rally in 1993. Some riders recalled that Mike emphasized at the start of that rally that the single most important thing about documenting bonus claims is to prove that you made the ride. Riders were told to be creative if obstacles prevented them from using customary approaches to prove that the ride to the bonus location had been made. A few riders contended that by adapting Garve's towel for the remainder of the rally, Tom was simply improvising to prove that he did ride to the bonus locations.

Controversy

In March 1996, I attended the annual Iron Butt Association Pizza Party in Daytona Beach. This event occurs during Bike Week, one of the major motorcycling events of the year. To make this Friday night event, I left Plano after work on Thursday and rode in freezing cold the entire 1,150 miles, non-stop, arriving 21 hours later. I arrived two hours before the party, checked

FINAL ADJUSTED STANDINGS

Standing	Rider	Miles Ridden	Points
1	Gary Eagan	12,266	19,992
2	Marty Jones	11,609	19,875
3	Martin Hildebrandt	9,736	17,982
4	Ron Major	11,227	17,369
5	Eugene McKinney	10,756	17,303
6	Ron Ayres	12,007	17,186
7	Michael Stockton	10,613	17,150
8	Morris Kruemcke	11,463	16,933
9	Kevin Donovan	9,930	16,769
10	Boyd Young	10,586	16,566
11	Harold Brooks	10,324	16,549
12	Roy Eastwood	11,550	16,530
13	Eddie Metz	11,217	16,460
14	Eric Faires	10,504	16,412
15	Jesse Pereboom	9,314	16,241
16	Bradley Hogue	11,098	15,806
17	Jerry Clemmons	9,984	15,527
18	Keith Keating	10,284	15,519
19	Gregg Smith	9,299	15,101
20	Horst Haak	9,548	14,951
21	Hank Rowland	9,559	14,951
22	Ed Otto	9,361	14,891
23	Jim Culp	9,480	14,695
24	Dennis Searcy	9,499	14,434
25	Michael Murphy	9,069	14,247
26	David Kerslake	9,072	14,167
27	Ed Fickess	9,809	14,152
28	William Thommes	8,935	14,077
29	Charles Elberfeld	10,313	14,009
30	Karol Patzer	9,593	14,003
31	Robert Ransbottom	8,971	13,652
32	Doug Stover	9,141	13,061
33	Frank Taylor	11,614	11,501
34	Rick Morrison	10,613	11,458
35	Mary Sue Johnson	9,156	10,567
36	Chuck Pickett	9,757	10,342
37	Ron & Karen McAteer	9,102	9,280

into a motel across the street from the pizza shop, and took a two-hour nap. Déjà vu.

When I walked across the street to the restaurant, more than 60 riders were present, including riders from previous rallies. Many, like Eddie Metz, Marty Jones, and Michael Stockton, did as I did and rode several thousand miles to have the opportunity to meet for only a few hours with their "Butt Buddies."

Murf flew in from St. Louis for the party. As riders were taking their places at the tables, he distributed copies of newspaper articles about his ride that had been published in the local newspapers a month after the rally. The headline of the article from the Sunday edition of the *St. Louis Post-Dispatch* was titled, "No Crash Diet: Biker Doctor Sheds 15 Lbs on 11,000-Mile Trek." The other, from the *Belleville* (Ill.) *Journal*, was titled "57-year-old biker takes a seat for 10,000-mile Iron Butt Rally." Both articles included photographs of murf seated on his motorcycle. In his tuxedo.

I expected to find Steve Chalmers at the party. He told me that he expected to arrive with a bullseye attached to his back. I assured him that for what it was worth, I wouldn't be silent about my feelings about the disqualifications if he was attacked or embarrassed at the event. Steve wasn't able to attend the party. I don't think he would have needed help in defending himself either.

During the party, Mike Kneebone rose to make a speech. He mentioned that, as all riders present knew, the 1995 event had been accompanied by several disqualifications. Mike went on to present a large trophy to Garve Nelson. The trophy was inscribed: "To the Oldest Rider Ever Disqualified from The Iron Butt Rally." A round of cheers went up for Garve. The trophy was supplied by one of Steve's critics. Mike awarded the trophy, fearing that presentation by one of Steve's critics would have contributed to rancor between members of the group.

I thought this ceremony was apropos and didn't consider it a demonstration against the disqualifications. I thought it provided a means for the riders to confirm their admiration for Garve in spite of his indiscretion.

Hank Rowland and Kathy Laidley at Morganton BMW Motorcycle Owners of America National Rally, July 1996. Hank served as co-chair of the rally, which was held in his home town. *Photo by Steve Cobern.*

After the rally, Dave Kerslake advised against trying to run the Iron Butt on a sport bike such as his Suzuki GSXR 1100.

Things flared up again when, at the end of March, Bob Higdon was asked in an e-mail from Tim Foreman at BMW Riders Association to comment on the reasons for the disqualifications. Bob's response, which was sent to members of a BMW Riders Association mailing list, was critical of the disqualifications. Bob defended Tom, Eddie, and Garve, and called for the disqualifications to be reversed.

I believe that Steve Chalmers's response to Bob's e-mail gave insight into his decision-making on the issue: "When you agree to stage an event, you also agree to enforce the rules of that event equally. I have known Garve for over 10 years, and he has been an inspiration to me as well as to others. And, as difficult as it was, if there was going to be a level playing field for all the riders, then the rules had to apply to Garve as well."

Steve concluded his response by writing, "The rallymaster has to put his own feelings aside and insure that there is a level playing field for all participants."

This started another round of e-mail from Steve's defenders. Finally, Mike Kneebone intervened as diplomat and peacemaker. His confirmation of the appropriateness of the disqualifications and his support for Steve's decision helped put the issue to rest. Mike stated in an e-mail message that Bob was unaware of some vital information when he issued his critical letter to Tim Foreman. He also pleaded for an end to the relentless barrage of e-mail. The appeal seemed to work.

10

Epilogue

Eighteen Months Later

Getting Hooked Up

While waiting in the parking lot for my appearance at the finish line, Barb overheard riders commenting that they felt behind on world events because it had been so long since they had been on-line. During the banquet immediately following the rally, Mike Kneebone remarked on the number of people who had been following Bob Higdon's daily rally reports published on CompuServe and other on-line forums.

Mike provided the Iron Butt web address (www.ironbutt.com), and I subscribed to an on-line service when I returned home. Before long, I was communicating with the small community of long distance riding enthusiasts on-line. Many Iron Butt veterans, as well as new riders awaiting their opportunity to participate in their first Iron Butt, keep the cyber-mailman busy with electronic conversation about the next rally. Much of that conversation involves veterans answering questions and dispensing advice, as well as good-natured ribbing about the next running of the event.

I found out several months later from one of my cyber-biking friends that a Yugo was once blown over the side of the bridge that occupied so much of my thoughts during those hours in Michigan. I shared that information with Gary Eagan, who understood my experience with the bridge, based on his crossing several hours before me. In spite of the spectacular sunset that he witnessed while on the bridge, Gary commented about how surprised he was at the appearance of the guard rails. He felt that he was looking down from his motorcycle at very low railings.

"What can I say about the Mackinaw Bridge?" Gary reported. "It's wonderful. Tall. Scary. That metal grating in the left lane is odd. I'm not accustomed to being able to see the lake through the road when the water is a couple of hundred feet below me."

Other Rallies

Endurance riding, though currently practiced by a very small percentage of motorcycle enthusiasts, is enjoying rapid growth in popularity and interest. By the time registration opened in early 1996 for the 1997 Iron Butt Rally, 313 entrants had completed applications and sent checks to vie for the 80 available slots. Although the Iron Butt is open to anyone, past competitors are given precedence in the series of drawings to choose the field. I was one of the lucky ones chosen to ride again in 1997. By the fall of 1996, the final list of competitors was published on the Iron Butt web site and mailed to contestants.

In the year after the 1995 Iron Butt Rally, I entered the Alberta 2000, the Utah 1088, MERA's Miles Inc., and MERA's 8/48. I was a qualified finisher in the Alberta 2000 and the Utah 1088 and finished third in Miles Inc., completing 2,639 miles in 36 hours.

The 8/48 rally calls for participants to ride through the lower 48 states in eight days or less. I was six days and 42 states into my ambitious plan to complete the ride in less than seven days when—once again—I lost my receipts. In this case, they provided proof of my entire ride to this point. No, they didn't blow out of my unzipped tank bag this time, but they were lost nonetheless. I was following the trail of Lewis and Clark through Idaho on my way to Clarkston, Washington. Washington would have been state number 43. I stopped for gas at a small station in Kooskia. It was raining and windy, and I was filling out my log sheets when I noticed another vehicle waiting for access to the pumps. Not wanting to make the driver wait, I placed my envelope of receipts and log sheet on top of the pump and pushed the motorcycle to the side of the station.

The next thing I remember is arriving receiptless in Clarkston. The trip back to Kooskia took several hours, and the receipts were gone, probably blown into the Clearwater River which parallels much of the Idaho route.

At the banquet at the end of the rally I received a special "Velcro Award." It reads, "Presented to Ron Ayres by the Motorcycle Endurance Rider Association for his uncanny ability to snatch defeat from the jaws of certain victory by losing his paperwork in two different rallies." Barb has some ideas about permanently attaching a receipt envelope to part of my anatomy for the 1997 Iron Butt. And the "Ayres Thing" has made its way into the vocabulary of the endurance riding community.

In addition to the 1997 Iron Butt, I've also entered the 1997 Utah 1088, Alberta 2000, Raw-Hide, and the 1998 Butt Buster.

Final Reflections
At the risk of being over-dramatic, I'll repeat something that Steve Chalmers said during the dinner on the eve of the rally: "This rally will change your life." Although I expected it to be a defining event in my life, I wasn't expecting anything so dramatic as a *change* in my life.

I've developed a deep feeling of camaraderie with my fellow riders. Since the rally, I have come to know many of them well. I also feel an attachment to those whom I haven't seen since. The Iron Butt isn't an easy rally to complete. Finishers and DNFers alike respect each other for having had the courage to attempt it.

Barb has often encouraged me to keep a diary of personal and business events, but I never had an inclination to do so until the Iron Butt. Then I felt compelled to do it, primarily for my personal use. Apparently this compulsion was shared by many of my fellow riders. When I asked them to share their personal experiences with me, I was surprised to learn that many of them had already developed written accounts.

In the months following the rally, I was surprised at the larger motorcycling community's level of interest. Written information is limited and many riders seem to have an insatiable appetite for more. I began to frequent the Iron Butt home page, Bob Higdon's home page, and a few other places of interest to motorcyclists. I discovered a lot of interest in endurance riding via e-mail. I now communicate with a number of riders on a regular basis.

Some evenings as I relax in my den, I'm overcome with satisfaction as I look at the endurance riding plaques, photographs, and other mementos on the walls. The photograph of the 1995 contestants, which I framed soon after the rally, is my favorite. It shows the finishers proudly displaying the commemorative coffee mugs they received during the banquet. Most riders are wearing their white Iron Butt T-shirts; one is wearing a tuxedo. There's a special look on their faces, a look that accompanies a great personal triumph, the sort of individual achievement that lasts a lifetime and that no one can ever take away. No matter the finishing position, they know that less than one rider in 50,000 can claim to have accomplished what they just have.

Most of the 38 faces are smiling, some partially concealed behind those in front of them, with five riders kneeling in the front row, their recently awarded trophies on the floor before them. The focal point of the photograph is Tom Loegering, kneeling on one knee, the shirt bearing the signatures of 55 fellow riders draped across the other. Tom is perhaps displaying the biggest smile of the group.

Eddie James is one of the few riders in the group whose lips are not parted by a wide smile. Instead, Eddie's look is one of quiet satisfaction. Although he didn't win the rally, having the second largest trophy of the day is enough for the moment.

I can only wonder how this photograph would look with Gary Eagan holding the winner's trophy and signed T-shirt, now in his possession. He rode more miles than any other rider. No one questioned the validity of the winning total of points that he earned. He deserves the trophy and I'm glad that he now has it.

The Riders – A Follow-Up

Leonard Aron

Leonard is entered in the 1997 Iron Butt. He's planning to have lobster in Maine—Martin Hildebrandt knows a great place. Leonard has sworn that if he finishes the 1997 rally with the 1946 Indian Chief, he will enter the 1999 rally with his 1932 Chief.

Steve Attwood

Steve is now trying to make a go of his own business in the motorcycling field. He owns Chilli Heated Clothing Limited in Bedfordshire, England.

"This means I get to make the tea and answer the phone as well as making the heated waistcoats," he reported. "At this time most of my sales come through adverts in the motorcycle press and word of mouth. European riders are still getting to learn about the benefits of heated clothing. The web page is working well and I also exhibit at shows and go along to club meetings to spread the word. The club meetings always go down well as I get to talk about the Iron Butt. I hope to expand into export markets as time progresses."

Harold Brooks

A veteran of the 1987, 1991, and 1993 Iron Butt rallies, Harold was back in Salt Lake City a year after the rally to compete in the Utah 1088.

Every October, Harold conducts his "Feast in the East" gathering in Forest, Virginia, which attracts riders from around the country. The 1996 event also attracted a large number of "newbies," those planning to compete in the Iron Butt for the first time in 1997, and welcoming the opportunity to meet veteran riders before the event.

Brian Bush

More than a year after the completion of the rally, Brian's video remains unfinished. The unexpected disqualifications rendered much of his work worthless. The substantial footage of Tom Loegering and Eddie James, shot both at the finishing line as well as at the awards banquet, was useless. And there wasn't enough available footage of Gary Eagan.

I spoke with Brian during Christmas week in 1996. He felt he was still several months away from having a revised video about the Iron Butt, rather than specifically about the 1995 event.

Jerry Clemmons

Of all of the riders in '95, none is more proud of his accomplishment than Jerry Clemmons. After Christmas 1995, I received a short letter and a photograph of him perched on one of his motorcycles, wearing his Christmas presents. His wife's sister and her husband's family presented him with a custom-made jacket and baseball-style hat. Both were embroidered with "Iron Butt 1995" and displayed his finishing position. In the letter, Jerry wrote: "I think they were trying to dress me up a little. They must have been tired of having me show up at dinner engagements wearing dress slacks and an Iron Butt T-shirt."

Jerry had packed a miniature tape recorder with him and made notes of his ride. Some time after the rally, he used the recordings to recall the details of his ride, and published a short article on the Iron Butt home page.

Jim Culp

Jim e-mailed me about a motorcycle trip he took nearly a year after the rally. "Last June, my son James and I went out and rode the SCMA Four Corners Tour together, just him and me sharing the bike for two weeks," he wrote. "That wasn't a feat of endurance, but it was a special experience for me, and I'm proud of it."

Jim's 1995 Iron Butt Rally towel is proudly displayed on his office wall in City Hall, Johnson City, Tennessee. "I do get a lot of nice comments about my towel on the wall," he wrote.

A member of MENSA, Jim Culp found that the Iron Butt Rally taxed his mental stamina as much as his physical endurance. A tired Jim is shown here shortly after the rally.

Gary Eagan

First place finisher Gary Eagan planned to participate in the Utah 1088 Rally in June 1996. Three weeks before the rally, he ran his motorcycle off a remote road in Utah at dawn and broke an arm and leg. He intentionally drove off the road to avoid deer standing in his path as he rounded a curve.

Gary came with crutches and casts to visit with the riders at the start of the Utah 1088. Although he wasn't able to compete in the rally, he won the grand prize for the third consecutive year for raising the most donations for Project Hope, receiving a two-week motorcycle vacation in Europe.

When I spoke to Gary almost five months after the accident, he was out of the casts but still limped a little. He wasn't able to bend his elbow or turn the palm of his hand parallel to either the floor or ceiling. His physician told him the arm had nearly required amputation.

He told me it was difficult to describe how badly he missed riding—enough that he began investigating having a motorcycle equipped with controls shaped to accommodate his injuries' limitations on his range of movement. Even with such modifications, the discomfort he will have to bear may limit him to 24- or 48-hour rallies.

In a letter dated mid-January 1997 he described his life as "an expensive medical novel."

"I had a total rebuild of my right wrist, arm, elbow, and shoulder on December 31. Recovery and rehabilitation time is about three months of intensive therapy, followed by another couple of months of semi-intensive work. If they don't get me pieced back together pretty soon, riding the '97 Butt may be difficult. If my right hand worked, I'd cross my fingers. I'm going to be hooked up to a machine designed to continuously flex my arm and bend my wrist virtually 24 hours a day. That will likely go on for nearly a month."

Gary is nonetheless entered in the 1998 Butt Buster.

Charles Elberfeld

When I asked Charles to tell me about his participation in the Iron Butt, he sent me some interesting observations and comments. In part, Charles wrote:

"I have thought a lot about the attitudes we all must have toward each other before, during, and after the rally. When I try to distance myself and look at the event, I think that the Iron Butt Rally is the neatest game anyone could ever come up with. Here are approximately 60 people ready to block off more than 11 days of their life to play a game with no time-outs, and minimal rules, and the equipment is maps, motorcycles, and the north American continent.

"The game only has significance and value to the participants, and the real value of it is contained within the interaction of the 'Butt Buddies'. I can only speak for my feelings but I think others may have traveled the same path. I want everyone to play, because that adds value to the event, but I want to do

Horst Haak, one of two Canadian riders entered in the 1995 Iron Butt
Rally, rode most of the rally with Hank Rowland.

better than everyone else, because it is a competition. I like
these people because we all have similar interests and work
ethics, and we all like to play hard.

"See you in Chicago next August."

Martin Hildebrandt

In a 1996 Christmas greeting, Martin reported that he
hadn't done much riding since the Iron Butt. He was preparing
to participate in the 1997 Iron Butt with a 163cc vintage two-
stroke Zündapp.

Horst Haak

Horst will be returning again in 1997 to participate in the
Iron Butt. He's also entered in the 1997 Alberta 2000.

Eddie James

Eddie is working for a Harley-Davidson dealership in St.
Paul, Minnesota. When I asked Mike Kneebone why Eddie's
and Tom Loegering's names were missing from the 1997 Iron
Butt entry list, he told me that, although preference is given to

veterans, their names hadn't been drawn. They are on the wait list and might replace riders who cancel.

Mike describes Tom and Eddie as dedicated endurance riding enthusiasts who, though embarrassed about what has happened, want to face their fellow riders and compete again. Whether he competes in the 1997 Iron Butt or not, Eddie is planning to deliver a 15-minute talk to the 1997 contestants about what *not* to do. I'm looking forward to seeing him there.

Eddie sponsored the second running of the Minnesota 1000 in the summer of '96. The rally, a miniature version of the Iron Butt, requires riders neither to travel 1,000 miles nor to stay in Minnesota. The rally takes place primarily in the 5 states surrounding Minnesota.

The rules included an odd twist. Before starting the rally, riders were required to turn in their drivers' license, which was sealed in an envelope and was returned to them. If they returned from the rally with the envelope still sealed, they would earn an additional 500 points. Of the 50 riders who participated in the rally, only two returned with their envelopes opened. One of them was the rally organizer, Eddie James.

Mary Sue Johnson

After her Iron Butt experience, fellow riders have begun calling Suzy "The Legend." Suzy patronizes In the Wind, a biker "grub and pub" on Cleveland Street in Griffith, Indiana. There is a picture of Suzy on her motorcycle on the wall. The photograph was taken by Sam Jones, a California photographer who captured the photo at the San Diego checkpoint. Sam was considerate enough to send Suzy several 8x10s.

When she asked owner Tom Hendricks why the photograph was placed so high on the wall, he told her that it was because the patrons hold her in such high regard. Tom wanted the photograph with the other "legends" whose photographs had been placed in the prominent location, including an old picture of Tom's father, Emmett, on a motorcycle and a photo of Walt Schwader, the recently deceased part-owner of the pub. Tom says he will never remove the photographs from the wall.

Suzy Johnson was one of only two women riding a Harley-Davidson, and the first woman ever to finish on one. This was Suzy's first motorcycle endurance riding event. *Photo by Sam Jones.*

Suzy wrote a short story about her experience in the Iron Butt for the *Hoosier Motorcyclist.* The article included the photograph of the finishers, taken after the banquet in Salt Lake City. The caption reads, "Why aren't these riders sitting down?" She has also been a guest speaker for the Rotary Club in Griffith.

Perhaps the most spectacular finish of the 1996 8/48 rally belongs to Suzy. She rode her Harley "Iron Butt Machine" to Denver nearly a week before the rally was to begin. The motorcycle was stolen from the parking lot of her motel two days before the start of the event. At least a dozen other Harleys were stolen that evening in the Denver area.

She had been considering purchasing a BMW, and took this opportunity to do it. She found one with a little over 1,000 miles on the odometer and purchased it on the spot. With less than 70 miles of experience riding it, she visited all 48 states in less than eight days to finish third in the rally.

Suzy is entered in the Iron Butt again in 1997 and is entered in the Butt Buster in 1998.

Marty Jones

Marty accompanied Eddie Metz to the annual pizza party in Daytona. Discussing his Iron Butt experience, he described waking up shortly after arriving home from the rally and jumping on his motorcycle, ready to ride another leg. Then he realized the rally was over. It was just as well, because his battery had gone dead.

I asked him if he was planning to participate in the 8/48 and he said that he believed the eight day format would require too much speed. He and Eddie came to the 8/48 for the pre-rally dinner to see the riders off, however. Marty is planning to run the Iron Butt again in 1997. He's also entered in the 1998 Butt Buster.

Ardys Kellerman

Fellow Rhode Islander Gregg Smith reported seeing Ardys several times as she recuperated from the injuries that she sustained during the rally. Ardys demolished her motorcycle and broke her left ankle and wrist.

"She first came into the shop in a wheel chair, then with a walker, and finally on the arm of one of her daughters," Gregg told me.

After her recovery, Ardys moved to Austin, Texas. She plans to participate in the Iron Butt again in 1997.

Morris Kruemcke

Morris will be back again for the 1997 rally. He's continuing to work on his Stealth Bike and may enter it. When I talked to him about a year after the 1995 rally, he was planning to put fuel injection and a few other refinements on the motorcycle.

He has also equipped his motorcycle with a cellular phone that he can use while on the move. During a recent trip to Canada one of his riding buddies wasn't able to join him. Morris teased him for not being able to get a "kitchen pass." As Morris was passing through Jasper in the Canadian Rockies he called his friend to advise him that it was a good thing he didn't make the trip.

"Why not?" his friend asked.

"Because the RCMP have a checkpoint set up. If you don't have a valid kitchen pass, they send you home," Morris chortled.

Morris swears that during the 1997 rally he'll be placing some calls from the road to Eddie Metz and other veterans who haven't entered.

Fritz and Phyllis Lang

I received a letter from Phyllis about a year after the rally. She reported that it still bothers her immensely not to have finished. Phyllis wrote, "It has been great meeting and getting to know some of the best riders in the world. All of you were great, especially Mike Kneebone. He has given me a lot of encouragement. Most other people just do not understand why anyone would attempt such a ride, especially more than once."

A year after the rally, Phyllis's Harley was rear-ended and totaled. She was riding again just a few days later.

The Langs aren't quitters. The 1997 rally will be their third attempt. Fritz had bypass surgery in August 1996 and is expecting to be in fine shape for the next rally. Neither Fritz nor Phyllis is planning to win, but both of them intend to finish.

Tom Loegering

Shortly after the disqualifications, I received a letter from Tom with a snapshot of him perched on a child's toy motorcycle. The snapshot had a caption about his preparedness for the next Iron Butt. The note also included a congratulatory comment acknowledging my sixth place finish.

The envelope included a reprint of a brief article from the newsletter of the BMW Club of Southern California. The editor's comments stated: "Though Tom can't say he is one of the six winners of the Iron Butt Rally, he can say he is the only rider ever disqualified from first place. Tom, a resident of Southern California, knows what it feels like to compete, finish well, win the rally, and be disqualified all in one race."

In the year following the rally, Tom rode his motorcycle through Chile and Argentina to Tierra Del Fuego, the southernmost point of South America, nearly within sight of Antarctica. After this 32 day trip, he competed in the Big Dog Ride through Colorado and Utah. The ride, sponsored by BMW of Denver, is billed as "The world's highest meanest dirtiest toughest BMW GS motorcycle ride."

While writing this book, I wrote to Tom to request details about his Iron Butt experience. In addition to the requested information, Tom shared his thoughts about his disqualification. He still believes it was unfair and contends that he is the rightful winner. With fewer than nine months to go before the 1997 Iron Butt Rally, Tom was one of many riders hoping that his name makes it from the waiting list to the entrant's list.

Steve Losofsky

Steve won the Miles Inc. rally in Nevada in July 1996 after logging 3,027 miles during the 36-hour rally. His business partner, Jan Cutler, finished in second place with 2,893 miles during the same period.

Steve also participated in the 8/48 rally. Although he didn't complete the rally, he provided a morning of amusement to the staff at Reno BMW when they heard him being interviewed by Bruce Van Dyke on KTHX, a local Reno radio station that Steve called as he was passing through Atlanta. After the interview, Steve called the shop to confirm that his friends at the shop had heard him.

It was nearly Christmas, 1996, when I saw a posting on the LDRIDER e-mail list announcing the 36-hour Raw-Hide endurance rally Reno BMW would be sponsoring the following July. This was followed by an announcement that Reno BMW would soon be planning additional endurance riding events.

Shortly after New Year's, I received e-mail from Jan Cutler:

Steve Losofsky had a stroke December 31 a.m., went critical about 6:00 p.m. and was given a 50-50 chance of making it through the ensuing 4-hour operation. It was expected that four to five days would be required before he would regain consciousness post op. And, it was questionable whether he would have significant impairment.

*The following afternoon he was carrying on a brief
conversation with Tom Almassy and me and wondering
when he could get back to work. The staff at St Mary's
hospital are talking "miracles." Could be, but, if you know
Steve . . . .*

It appears that Steve will have a successful recovery, but he
won't be competing in the 1997 Iron Butt. This time it's Jan
Cutler's turn again. Jan is also entered in the 1998 Butt Buster.

Ron Major

Even before the 1995 Iron Butt Rally, Ron Major had participated in more rallies than most endurance riders. The list
includes the Nevada 1100, several SaddleSore 1000s, the Cal 24
Hour Rally, *seven* Southern California Motorcycle Association
(SCMA) Blazing Saddle rides, *five* Utah 1088 rallies (including
a first place finish in 1992), *five* Cal 1+1 Rallies, Bite the Bullet,
the SCMA Four Corners Tour, and the Three Flags Classic.

In September 1996, Ron won the MERA 8/48 Rally sponsored by Steve Chalmers. He's planning to participate in the
1997 Iron Butt Rally and admits that he would like to be the
first rider to win *two* Iron Butts. He acknowledges that the feat
is becoming increasingly unlikely as the field of experienced
riders continues to grow.

Ron is also entered in the 1998 Butt Buster.

Ron and Karen McAteer

Ron and Karen qualified as finishers and entered Iron Butt
history as the first couple to complete the rally riding two-up.
Their delay in reaching the final checkpoint prevented them
from celebrating their accomplishment with their fellow riders.

Eddie Metz

I visited with Eddie when he came to the kickoff of the 8/48
Rally in Denver in 1996. He later mailed a copy of his written
account of the 1995 Iron Butt Rally to me to help in writing this
book.

Eddie doesn't plan to run the Iron Butt Rally again, but is
entered in the 1998 Butt Buster.

Rick Morrison

Rick participated in the 8/48 and is entered again in the 1997 Iron Butt. He's also entered in the 1998 Butt Buster.

Mike Murphy

The riding community owes a lot to murf. There couldn't be a better ambassador to the endurance riding community's best known rally. Murf's participation added an air of legitimacy to the rally, and every description of the rally that I have seen (or written myself) mentions that the field ranges "from neurosurgeons to lawyers" or "from hard-core bikers to neurosurgeons." The description always includes neurosurgeons.

More than a year had passed when I asked murf about his introduction to motorcycling. "I first started in 1992," he said. "My mother wouldn't let me have a motorcycle or a BB gun. She died. Now I have 4 motorcycles. I still don't have a BB gun."

When I asked him to share his thoughts about the rally, he reported that his first recollection was about two hours into it when he was going through southern Idaho and realized the enormity of the projected ride. He began to appreciate the fellowship of the other riders as they met at the checkpoints. As the rally wore on, he appreciated the immensity of the United States and the friendliness of the people.

"Since the completion of the rally, I've received countless letters and Christmas cards from the participants. To say the least, lasting friendships have been forged. And attending the annual pizza party in Daytona was like visiting family."

At the end of his message murf wrote, "I know this was brief but I actually get a little choked up writing about the Iron Butt. Like the 'Swamp Thing' says: 'This is a signal event in your life.' One interesting aside is the incidental opportunity to spread the motorcycling gospel to many groups that ordinarily would not be exposed: The local Rotary Club, travel club, and the St. Clair County Medical Society."

Ed Otto

Ed Otto finished in 22nd position, ahead of 15 other finishers and 14 DNFs. He accomplished what many, including Bob Higdon, thought was impossible on a Helix. The accomplish-

Epilogue   219

ment received a lot of publicity in the months following the rally, including extensive coverage in *Motorcycle Consumer News.*

Ed will share Rallymaster duties with Mike Kneebone in 1997. The rally will begin and end near their homes in Chicago.

Karol Patzer

After completing the Iron Butt, Karol documented her first 1,000-mile SaddleSore with a 21-hour ride from her home in Eagan, Minnesota, to the BMW MOA gathering in Morganton, North Carolina—a distance of almost 1,200 miles. Although she had ridden 1,000-mile days before this, she had never documented them. Immediately after the Morganton event, she completed the "Bun Burner" 1,500 with a ride from Knoxville, Tennessee, to Gunnison, Colorado—precisely 1,500 miles in 36 hours.

Karol also spoke of her Iron Butt experience at a Motorcycle Safety Conference and at the BMW MOA National conference. In recognition for her participation in the Iron Butt, the BMW MOA, and Women on Wheels, Karol rode the kick-off leg of the '96 Pony Express Rally, an honor that she described as the highlight of the '96 season for her.

The last time I spoke to Karol, she joked that one of the things that she loves about being with the riders is that it's the only time that she can be in the same room with 50 other people who don't think she's nuts. She also confided that her "significant other" was about to throw her out because he was tired of worrying whether or not she'd survive her trips.

Jesse Pereboom

Jesse wrote to me, after the rally, that it took enough out of him that he probably won't be doing much long distance riding for a while.

"It has now been almost five months since the end of the rally, and slowly the urge to actually get on my bike and go somewhere is starting to come back. However, once I get to the grocery store I decide I've had enough and turn around and come back home."

Immediately after the rally, Jesse moved to Phoenix to study at the Motorcycle Mechanics Institute. He plans to finish in the spring of 1997. He will then have a certification from Harley-Davidson and will be looking for a job in the Minneapolis area to be closer to his girlfriend.

Hank Rowland

Hank, who decided early in the rally to ride with Horst Haak, finished with exactly the same 14,951 points as Horst, tying for 20th place.

I saw Hank almost a year after the Iron Butt in Salt Lake City at the running of the Utah 1088. He and Harold Brooks came west for the rally together. On the way home, Hank's rear drive seized while he was doing 80 mph, scaring the life out of him and nearly causing him to fall. This was the result of neglecting to torque down the drain plug on the rear end of his K100RT. The plug had fallen out, along with the lubricants.

Hank was ready to rent a truck to get the bike home, at a cost of about $600. Harold suggested that he buy a used pickup truck, which he did. He charged the truck to his credit card and sold it for what he had paid when he returned to Morganton.

Hank was co-chair for the BMW MOA National Rally in his home town of Morganton, North Carolina. The event attracted 6,000 attendees and 5,000 motorcycles from all over the world and resulted in a lot of good press for motorcycling in that part of the country. Hank received certificates of appreciation for his efforts by both the BMW MOA and the local Chamber of Commerce.

I heard from Hank again on Thanksgiving 1996. Just a week earlier he swerved to avoid a 77-year-old who ran a red light, causing Hank to drop and total his K100. Hank reported that he was sore, rashed, and bruised but otherwise unharmed.

Hank also reported that he had recently acquired a '95 K1100LT and was rebuilding it. It had been wrecked, but he was able to acquire it for the right price.

Richard Shrader

The 1995 Iron Butt Rally was "Swamp Thing's" third, but he has yet to complete one. He has done well in other rallies, including one of the early Utah 1088s in which he finished third.

Gregg Smith, after his fourth Iron Butt Rally in 1995, has completed more Iron Butts than any other rider. *Photo by Ginger Denneny.*

In the mid '70s, he once finished third in a Cal 1,000 Rally in which nearly 2,500 motorcyclists competed.

Rick's license was suspended for two months due to the traffic violation that he was charged with on the first night of the rally in Nebraska. Because he lost his license, he was forced to cancel his trip to the FIM rally in North Africa, forfeiting his entrance fees, camping fees, and ferry fees. He has now equipped his motorcycle with jammers facing front and rear.

I received a Christmas card from him with a photograph of his wife Jean and his two wolves covered with snow, sitting in one of his sidecar-equipped motorcycles in the front of his house in Oregon. One of the wolves, Sasha, is now 14 years old. Rick has had her since she was only five months old.

He is entered in the 1997 Iron Butt and expects to have earned BMW's 400,000-mile award by the time the rally is held. He is also entered in the 1998 Butt Buster.

Gregg Smith

Gregg set the all-time record for the greatest number of Iron Butt finishes. He finished in 1986, 1991, 1993, and 1995. With more than 40,000 rally miles to his credit, Gregg also holds the record for the most miles ridden by a single person in the Iron Butt rallies. He plans to participate again in 1997, but suggests that this may be his last Iron Butt.

After the rally, Gregg moved from Rhode Island to Florida and joined the American Motorcycle Institute (AMI) in Daytona. When I spoke to Gregg during the 1996 Christmas season, he was trying to locate a large facility to accommodate the Iron Butt annual gathering in March.

Frank Taylor

Shortly after the rally, Frank Taylor's motorcycle was stolen. Frank hadn't replaced it by the time of the Utah 1088 in the summer of '96, so he and his wife, Jessica, volunteered to operate the Delta, Utah, checkpoint. When I passed through at 1:00 a.m., I appreciated the cookies Jessica had baked for distribution to the riders.

Willie Thommes

Willie and his border collie, Dexter, made the 3,300-mile "southerly route" trip from Spokane to Daytona to attend the Iron Butt Pizza Party in March 1996. Willie dressed Dexter in a sweater and leather cape before heading for Florida in the freezing cold.

Willie competed in the Utah 1088 in the summer of 1996— with Dexter between the handlebars. Dexter, the first dog to complete the Utah 1088, was invited to the banquet after the rally. I was honored to have them as dinner companions.

Willie plans to compete again in the 1997 Iron Butt. He'll be riding a BMW R1100RT that he acquired as a Christmas present in 1996. He considered letting Dexter accompany him, but doesn't think he'll be able to find dog-friendly motels on short notice.

Boyd Young

Boyd attended the annual Iron Butt Pizza Party in Daytona in 1996. He is president of the Honda Sport Touring Association (HSTA) in Oklahoma and has invited Mike Kneebone to speak at one of the club's gatherings in June 1997. Mike will be hosting a meeting for new riders of the 1997 Iron Butt Rally in Muskogee and has agreed to address HSTA.

Boyd is planning to participate in the 1997 Iron Butt Rally.

Other Players

Steve Chalmers

Because the Iron Butt Rally takes place only every other year, Steve stages another long rally on alternate years. In 1994 it was the five-day Run What Ya Brung Rally. In the summer of 1996, he hosted the 8/48, which calls for riders to visit all 48 contiguous states in eight days or less.

For 1998, he has planned an 11-day Butt Buster that will criss-cross the United States and will have a higher base mileage than the Iron Butt. By mid-January 1997, it appeared that the 40 slots would be filled quickly.

The brief biography that Mike Kneebone wrote about Steve in the list of 1997 Iron Butt competitors states, in part: "Not everyone loves Steve, but you can bet that when you enter one of his events, you are going to be treated fairly!"

Steve is looking forward to the 1997 Iron Butt Rally and to his own Butt Buster as a competitor.

Bob Higdon

At the conclusion of the rally, Bob was planning a 20-month trip around the world on a 1986 BMW R80/GS. Bob has his own home page on the Internet (www.ironbutt.com/higindx.html) and plans to use it to report his progress. Wanting to be sure repairs wouldn't delay him on his world tour, he enrolled in the American Motorcycle Institute in 1994, graduated from the 5-month program, and is now a certified BMW mechanic.

One Saturday morning a few weeks before Christmas in 1996, I read Bob's "The View From The Bunker" column in the November issue of *On The Level*. The article was about Bob's attendance at the funeral of a rider who had been killed in a motorcycle accident in October. Later that same day, I received e-mail from Mike Kneebone. Mike had just talked to Bob, who was in a Mexican hospital recovering from surgery necessitated by a motorcycle accident.

During the first weeks of January, 1997 Bob sent e-mail in response to my note inquiring about his progress in recuperating from his injuries.

"Once I stopped flying through the air my recovery went surprisingly well," he wrote. He went on to question, "What's going on here?" after reflecting on the recent deaths of four motorcyclists who were all younger than him. He referred to Gary Eagan, who "probably will never ride again."

I responded with e-mail telling Bob of my recent telephone conversation with Gary, during which he confirmed his intention to compete in the 1997 rally. Bob's next message demonstrated that he maintained his wit during his convalescence:

"You know my predictive ability: Otto won't finish, Eagan's in the toilet after leg #1, Ayres is joining him there soon, etc. From what I hear, Gary will be lucky to ever sit on a motorcycle again, much less ride one. For once, I hope I'm wrong."

Mike Kneebone

Mike has been occupying himself with the expansion of the Iron Butt home page on the Internet and with planning the largest Iron Butt Rally ever. The 1997 event is scheduled to include 80 participants.

A

1995 Iron Butt Rally Entrants

Entry	Rider	Age	Home	Occupation	Motorcycle
1	Ron Ayres	52	Plano, Texas	Sales Management	'95 BMW K1100LT
2	Bradley Hogue	47	Aurora, Colorado	Systems Development	'93 Honda Gold Wing
3	Garve Nelson	72	San Leandro, California	Retired Motorcycle Dealer	'83 Honda Ascot
4	Leonard Aron	47	Ventura, California	Attorney	'46 Indian Chief
5	Steve Attwood	38	Bedfordshire, England	Management Consultant	'83 Moto Guzzi
6	Ron Major	53	Temple City, California	Television Engineer	'94 Honda ST1100
7	Eric Steven Faires	32	Memphis, Tennessee	Attorney	'93 BMW K1100LT
8	Michael Murphy	55	Belleville, Illinois	Neurosurgeon	'93 Honda ST1100
9	Roy Eastwood	51	Ontario, Canada	Airline Service Leader	'94 BMW R1100RS
10	Jim Culp	42	Johnson City, Tennessee	Attorney	'94 Honda Gold Wing
11	Phyllis Lang	57	Sewickley, Pennsylvania	Administrative Manager	'94 Harley-Davidson FXR
12	Fritz Lang	57	Sewickley, Pennsylvania	Constable	'79 Honda Silver Wing
13	Brian Bush	?	Corpus Christi, Texas	Video Productions	'88 BMW K100LT
14	Gary Gottfredson	58	Sandy, Utah	Bakery Owner	'91 BMW K100RS
15	Bob Honemann	46	Chicago, Illinois	Motorcycle Dealer	'65 BMW R60/2

Entry	Rider	Age	Home	Occupation	Motorcycle
16	Rick Morrison	40	Leavenworth, Washington	Flight Attendant	'94 BMW R100RT
17	Gregg Smith	46	Providence, Rhode Island	Motorcycle Sales	'87 Yamaha Venture
18	Skip Ciccarelli	45	Athol, Massachusetts	Carpenter	'86 Cal II Moto Guzzi
19	Charles Elberfeld	41	Mentor, Ohio	Nuclear Plant Operations	'94 BMW K75SA
20	Martin Jones	32	San Angelo, Texas	Law Enforcement Officer	'92 Kawasaki Voyager
21	Morris Kruemcke	57	Houston, Texas	Sales Representative	'89 Honda Gold Wing
22	Ed Otto	43	Chicago, Illinois	Insurance Agent	'95 Honda Helix
23	Eddie Metz	36	Grapevine, Texas	Airline Mechanic	'85 Honda Gold Wing
24	Thomas Loegering	55	Manhattan Beach, CA	Real Estate Management	'95 BMW R1100GS
25	Thomas Loegering, Jr.	26	Manhattan Beach, CA	Real Estate Management	'85 BMW K100RS
26	Ken Hatton	46	Chicago, Illinois	Projectionist	'91 Kawasaki ZX-11
27	Robert Fairchild	40	San Jose, California	Electronics	'91 Honda Gold Wing
28	Martin Hildebrandt	28	Stadthagen, Germany	Owner, Software Company	'93 Honda ST1100
29	Rick Shrader	49	Redmond, Oregon	Electrician	'94 BMW R1100RS
30	Doug Stover	48	Santa Rosa, California	Human Resources	'88 Honda Gold Wing
31	Harold Brooks	53	Forest, Virginia	Model Maker	'84 Honda Gold Wing
32	Steve Losofsky	43	Sparks, Nevada	Owner, BMW Dealership	'86 BMW K100RS
33	Kevin P. Donovan	36	Painesville, Ohio	Nuclear Qual. Assurance	'94 Honda GL1500A
34	Ardys Kellerman	61	Providence, Rhode Island	Computers	'94 BMW K75RT
35	Gary J. Eagan	46	Salt Lake City, Utah	Financial Advisor	'94 BMW K1100LT
36	Horst K. Haak	56	Ontario, Canada	Risk Management	'95 BMW K1100RS

Entry	Rider	Age	Home	Occupation	Motorcycle
37	Jesse Pereboom	24	Webster, South Dakota	Motorcycle Mechanic	'93 Harley-Davidson FLHT
38	Dennis Searcy	45	Angleton, Texas	Boilermaker/ Welder	'85 Harley-Davidson FLT
39	Frank Taylor	56	Salt Lake City, Utah	Finance Manager	'93 Yamaha FJ1200
40	William Thommes	50	Spokane, Washington	Owner, Ped Home Care	'91 Harley-Davidson FXRP
41	Robert Ransbottom	39	New Bedford, Massachusetts	Sales	'91 BMW K75RT
42	Chuck Pickett	53	Bridgeville, Pennsylvania	Computer Equipment Sales	'90 Honda Gold Wing
43	Ron & Karen McAteer	59/ 53	Fairview Heights, Illinois	Retired	'94 Honda ST1100
44	Michael Stockton	40	Mustang, Oklahoma	Plant Technician	'93 BMW K1100LT
45	Eugene McKinney	50	West Point, Mississippi	School Teacher	'94 BMW R1100RS
46	Mary Sue Johnson	56	Griffith, Indiana	Truck Driver	'93 Harley Davidson
47	Karol Patzer	47	Eagan, Minnesota	Sales Specialist	'88 BMW K75C
48	Keith Keating	45	Bethal, Connecticut	Motorcycle Policeman	'94 BMW R1100RS
49	David Kerslake	31	Howard City, Michigan	Farm Worker	'94 Suzuki GSXR 1100
50	Ed Fickess	48	Pittsburgh, Pennsylvania	–	'89 Yamaha Venture
51	Hank Rowland	60	Morgantown, North Carolina	Home Lighting Manufacturer	'86 BMW K100RT
52	Boyd Young	33	Atoka, Oklahoma	Restaurant Owner	'91 BMW K100RS
53	Jerry Clemmons	47	Gastonia, North Carolina	Partner, Retail Paint	'84 Honda Gold Wing
54	Kevin Mello	25	New Bedford, Massachusetts	Sales	'93 BMW K1100LT
55	Eddie James	31	Minneapolis, Minnesota	Motorcycle Manager	'93 BMW K1100RS

B

Bonus Locations

Leg 1 "Opportunities" – Salt Lake City, Utah, to Spokane, Wash.	Points
Anchorage, Alaska	963
Chimney Rock Historical Site, Nebraska	315
Las Vegas, Nevada	286
Lincoln Monument, Wyoming	247
Territorial Prison, Rawlins, Wyoming	199
Rocky Mountain National Park, Colorado	182
Seattle/Tacoma International Airport	137
Railroad Museum, Helper, Utah	86
Steamboat Springs, Colorado	49
Dinosaur National Monument, Vernal, Utah	47
Arches National Park, Utah	43
Bryce Canyon National Park, Utah	42
Winnemucca, Nevada	29
Wendover, Nevada	28
Grand Teton National Park	27
Vernal, Utah	26
Glacier National Park, Montana	23
Golden Spike National Historical Site, Utah	21
Craters of the Moon National Monument, Idaho	19
Lolo, Montana	18
Jackson, Wyoming	16
Lewiston, Idaho	13
Salmon, Idaho	11
Boise, Idaho	7

Spokane window opens: 3:00 p.m.
Checkpoint bonus: 2,000 points
Spokane window closes: 5:00 p.m.
Penalty for arriving late: 1 point per minute

Leg 2 "Prospects" – Spokane, Wash., to San Diego, Calif.	Points
Washington, DC	643
Custer Battlefield National Monument	413
Death Valley National Monument	283
Golden Gate Bridge, San Francisco, California	268
Buffalo, Wyoming	136
Cycle Logical BMW, Eugene, Oregon	83
Reno BMW, Sparks, Nevada	69
South Valley Yamaha, Sandy, Utah	68
Lassen National Park	67
Yosemite National Park, California	59
Tonopah, Nevada	54
Cabrillo National Monument, California	51
Klamath Falls, Oregon	47
Toll Bridge, Hood River, Oregon	38
San Juan Capistrano, California	33
Winnemucca, Nevada	31
Crater Lake National Park	23
Los Angeles, California	23
San Diego International Airport	12
The Dalles, Oregon	11

San Diego window opens: 10:00 a.m.
Checkpoint bonus: 2,250 points
San Diego window closes: 12:00 p.m.
Penalty for arriving late: 1 point per minute

Leg 3 "Possibilities" – San Diego, Calif., to Ft. Lauderdale, Fla.	Points
Mount Rushmore National Park, South Dakota	687
Brownsville, Texas	434
Lebanon, Kansas	363
Torrey, Utah	341
Meteor Crater, Arizona	168
Dr. Pepper Museum, Waco, Texas	162
Gasparilla Island Toll Bridge, Florida	147
Great Smokey Mountain National Park	141
Gatlinburg, Tennessee	111
Canon City, Colorado	103
Durango, Colorado	99
Laughlin, Nevada	92
Spaceport Visitors Center, Cape Canaveral	89
Coronado Bridge, San Diego	87
Grand Canyon, Arizona (North Rim)	87
Everglades Parkway, Florida	86
Jackson, Mississippi	81
Central City, Colorado	74
Carlsbad Caverns, New Mexico	72
Billy the Kid's Grave, Fort Sumner, New Mexico	72
The Alamo, San Antonio, Texas	61
Keyenta, Arizona	41
Zion National Park, Utah	36
Grand Canyon, Arizona (South Rim)	34
South Fork Ranch, Dallas, Texas	27
Pensacola, Florida	21
Panama City, Florida	21
Amarillo, Texas	19
Fort Worth, Texas	18
USS Alabama, Mobile, Alabama	18
Needles, California	17
Shreveport, Louisiana	15

Ft. Lauderdale window opens: 6:00 p.m.
Checkpoint bonus: 2,500 points
Ft. Lauderdale window closes: 7:00 p.m.
Penalty for arriving late: 5 points per minute

Leg 4 "Challenges" – Ft. Lauderdale, Fla. to Gorham, Maine	Points
Fort Kent, Maine	714
Grand Isle Bridge, Buffalo, New York	613
Chesapeake Bay Bridge Tunnel	513
Margaritaville Bar, Key West, Florida	389
Jamestown, Virginia	379
Cape Cod, Massachusetts	369
Beaver Tail State Park, Rhode Island	307
Biltmore Mansion, Asheville, North Carolina	278
Gettysburg, Pennsylvania	273
Bluefield, West Virginia	247
Parkersburg, West Virginia	237
New Haven, Connecticut	199
Charleston, South Carolina	158
Appomattox, Virginia	149
Everglades Parkway, Florida	141
Fort Meyers, Florida	122
Charleston, West Virginia	118
Fort Pulaski National Monument, Georgia	52
Dover, Delaware	39
St. George Island Road, Florida	14
Savannah, Georgia	13

Gorham window opens: 6:00 p.m.
Checkpoint bonus: 2,750 points
Gorham window closes: 8:00 p.m.
Penalty for arriving late: 10 points per minute

Leg 5 "Obstacles" – Gorham, Maine, to Salt Lake City, Utah	Points
Blaine, Washington	2,485
Venice, Louisiana	1,839
Hayward, Wisconsin	816
Mackinaw City, Michigan	701
Denver, Colorado	586
Lafayette and Dover, Tennessee	584
Loveland, Colorado	491
Glenshaw, Pennsylvania	486
Minot, North Dakota	463
Pikes Peak, Colorado	452
Mena, Arkansas	379
Motorcycle Museum, Westerville, Ohio	354
Newport Toll Bridge, Newport, Rhode Island	291
Fort Clark, Bismark, North Dakota	291
Colorado Springs, Colorado	281
Fort Knox, Kentucky	269
Yellowstone National Park, Wyoming	268
Jack Daniels Distillery, Lynchburg, Tennessee	263
Theodore Roosevelt National Park, North Dakota	263
Scobey, Montana	242
Hot Springs National Park, Little Rock, Arkansas	219
Fort Collins, Colorado	213
Scottsbluff, Nebraska	201
Des Moines, Iowa	196
Kansas Turnpike	189
Joplin, Missouri	189
Wayne, Indiana	184
Gunnison, Colorado	181
Sherman Mountains Sign, Wyoming	173
Springfield, Illinois	167
Brattleboro, Vermont	162
Bowling Green, Kentucky	147
Daniel Boone Parkway, Kentucky	141
Daniel Boone Homestead, Reading, Pennsylvania	117

Salt Lake City window opens: 5:00 p.m.
Checkpoint bonus: 3,000 points
The fat lady sings: 7:00 p.m.
Penalty for arriving late: 10 points per minute

Index

About the Author

Ron Ayres, a nationally recognized motorcycle endurance rider, is a member of the Motorcycle Endurance Riding Association (MERA) and the Iron Butt Association. He has competed in such internationally recognized events as the Iron Butt Rally, the Alberta 2000, the Utah 1088, Miles, Inc., and the 8/48.

He finished the 1995 Iron Butt Rally in sixth place and finished second for distance traveled, logging more than 12,000 miles in 11 days. This accomplishment earned him the 10/10ths Challenge Award for traveling more than 1,000 miles per day for ten consecutive days, an honor bestowed upon few endurance riders.

When not competing in endurance events, Ron is a division vice president of an information technology company based in Plano, Texas, where he and Barbara make their home.